To Pa

Merry Christmas 2005

Love, Jaden Thomas

" Lets read together ! "

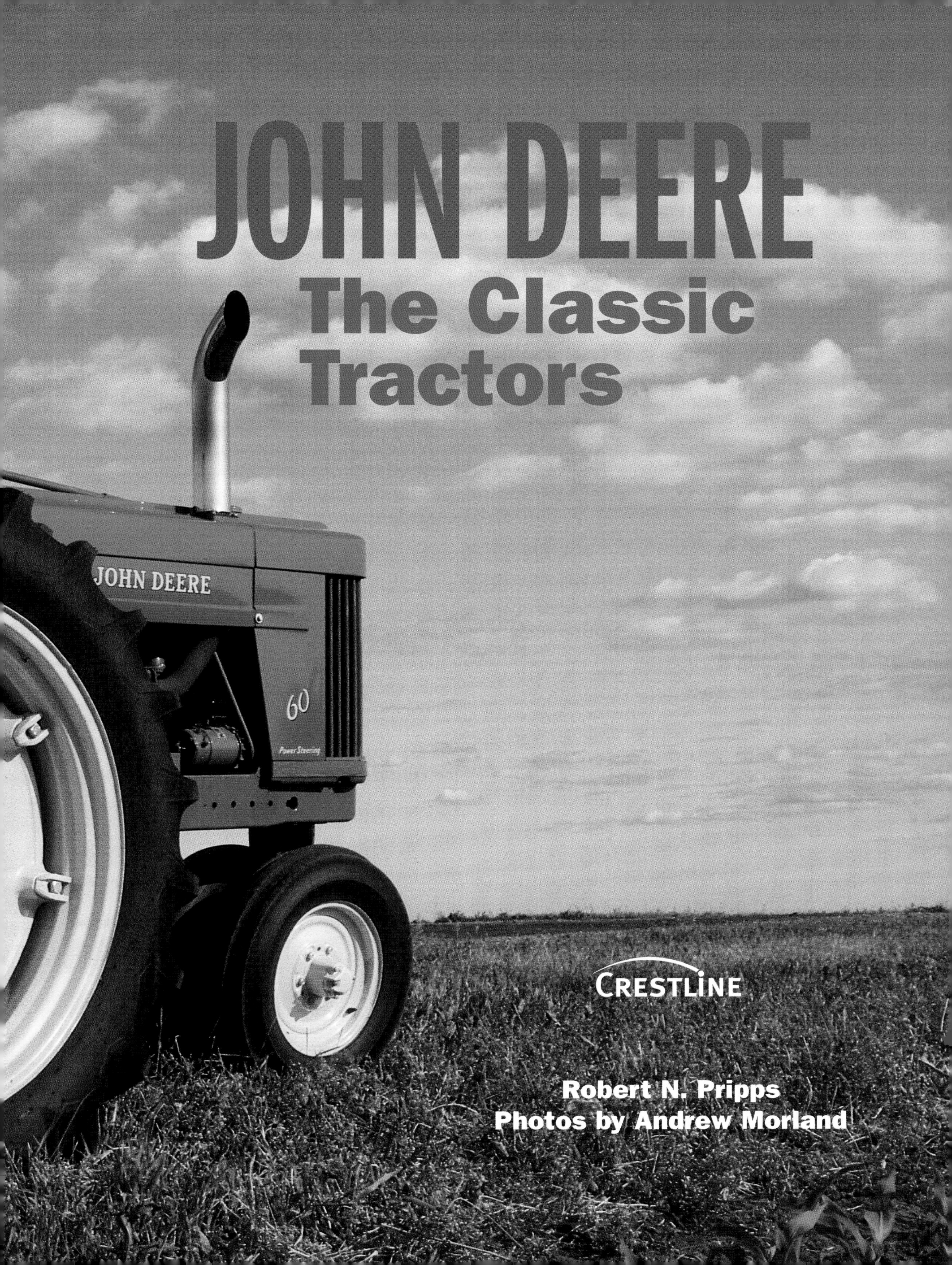

# JOHN DEERE
## The Classic Tractors

JOHN DEERE

60

Power Steering

CRESTLINE

**Robert N. Pripps**
**Photos by Andrew Morland**

First published in 1994. This edition published in 2005 by Crestline, an imprint of MBI Publishing Company, Galtier Plaza, Suite 200, 380 Jackson Street, St. Paul, MN 55101-3885 USA.

MBI titles are also available at discounts in bulk quantity for industrial or sales-promotional use. For details write to Special Sales Manager at MBI Publishing Company, Galtier Plaza, Suite 200, 380 Jackson Street, St. Paul, MN 55101-3885 USA.

ISBN-13: 978-0-7603-2344-1
ISBN-10: 0-7603-2344-5

Editor: Lindsay Hitch

Printed in China

*About the Author*
Robert N. Pripps was born on a small farm in northern Wisconsin in 1932. He retired from his first career in the aviation industry at age 55. He then began a second career writing about historic and collectable tractors. Bob has authored 25 books on tractors and has owned a variety of tractors over the years. He currently uses a restored Ford-Ferguson and a Massey 85 work tractor on his 55-acre maple syrup operation that is part of the farm on which he was born.

*About the Photographer*
Andrew Morland is the one of the world's most prolific tractor photographers, having contributed photos to more than 22 books, including *Ford Tractors, Big Green: John Deere GP Tractors, Fordson Tractors, Allis-Chalmers Tractors, Modern Farm Tractors, Farmall Tractors,* and *Massey Tractors.* He resides in Somerset, England.

*On the front cover*
The John Deere Model 60 was built from 1952 to 1956 as the successor to the famous Model A. Although the one shown is a 37-year-old antique, a more handsome tractor would be difficult to find. The 35 belt-horsepower-rated Model 60 is also as capable as many "modern" tractors. Owner Rich Ramminger, of Morrisonville, Wisconsin, used this one for plowing the year this photo was taken (1992).

*On the frontispiece*
For the serious antique tractor collector, the serial number is the important thing. This allows, first of all, for recognition of a rare, or unique, version of an otherwise common machine. Secondly, it allows the collector to determine the unit's original configuration for accurate restoration. Shown here is Bruce Keller's 1938 John Deere BWH, one of only 50 made.

*On the title page*
Rich Ramminger's John Deere Model 60 was built in 1956. Prior to restoration, Ramminger won a "Slow Race" with it. The chrome exhaust stack slips over the stock muffler and is only for looks. This is a gasoline version of the successor to the historic John Deere Model A. All-fuel and LPG versions of the Model 60 were also available.

*On the back cover*
(Top) Here's a great Model B general-purpose tractor—the very first, serial number 1000. It is one of several "first editions" owned by the Kellers of Forest Junction, Wisconsin. The John Deere B was essentially a scale model of the A, although there are subtle differences between the two in design details. (Bottom) Although over 30 years old, the 630 is still much in demand by farmers for routine farm chores. A new 40- to 50-horsepower tractor would cost three to four times as much as a good refurbished 630. Plus, with the 630, you get the distinctive sound of the two-cylinder engine. This 630 is owned by Orv Rothgarn, of Owatonna, Minnesota, who has a collection of 23 John Deere tractors.

# Contents

A 1933 John Deere GPWT with over-the-top steering, owned by Bruce and Walter Keller of Forest Junction, Wisconsin. This one is serial number 405135.

# Acknowledgments

My thanks and appreciation go to the following people who helped immeasurably in making this pictorial history possible:  First of all, to Andrew Morland; without his excellent photographs this book would be hard to sell!

Next, to helpful equipment companies:

Meridian Implement, my Rockford, Illinois, John Deere dealer.

Polacek Implement, Phillips, Wisconsin, who did the work on my John Deere B.

And to Deere & Company; especially Dr. Leslie Stegh and Ms. Vicki Eller in the Deere Archives and Records Services Department.

Thanks to the following tractor collectors who generously gave of their time and energies to provide information and photo opportunities for this book. Despite their best efforts, some of their tractors did not get photographed because of weather and scheduling difficulties. In other cases, due to circumstances beyond their control, pictures taken do not appear in this book; for these omissions, we heartily apologize. For those that do appear, the pictures speak for themselves as to the loving dedication of the owners to their hobby. Andrew Morland and myself, as well as the staff and management of MBI Publishing Company, extend our thanks to the following collectors:

Lyle Pals, Egan, Illinois; Rich Ramminger, Morrisonville, Wisconsin; Walter and Bruce Kellor, Forest Junction, Wisconsin; Orv Rothgarn, Owatonna, Minnesota; Jim Quinn, East Peoria, Illinois; Bruce Johnson, Maple Park, Illinois; Clarence (Bunky) Meese, Freeport Illinois; and Jim Kenney, Streater, Illinois.

# Introduction

The words "John Deere," like the word "Tahiti," conjure a mental image complete with sounds, smells, and feelings. Especially to the older agriculturist, the included sound bite is one with the distinctive music of a laboring two-cylinder tractor engine. It is our intention to add to the visual image through the pictures in this book.

Photographer Andrew Morland and I traveled the states of Wisconsin, Minnesota, and Illinois to photograph the beautifully restored historic tractors appearing in the following pages. In the text, I have attempted to infuse the tempo of the times into the history of the John Deere company and its general-purpose tractors. These were times, as they say, to try men's souls. They were also times of gifted men, both in the industry and on the farm.

This book includes only John Deere general-purpose tractors simply to limit its scope and so to concentrate on the general, or all-purpose, concept in tractors born in the late Twenties. The definition is stretched to include the utility concept of the Forties.

This is my second book on John Deere tractors (the first was *John Deere Two-cylinder Tractor Buyer's Guide*, also published by MBI Publishing Company). I hope it will not be my last. My associations with Deere & Company, its tractors, and the John Deere tractor collectors have only served to heighten my already high regard for the great green and yellow machines.

—*Robert N. Pripps*

# Chapter One

# EASING INTO
# THE TRACTOR
# BUSINESS

A replica of the 1892 Froelich tractor stands in the display building at the Deere & Company headquarters. John Froelich started the company that later produced the Waterloo Boy tractor. In 1918, Deere & Company entered the tractor business by acquiring the company. *Author Collection*

## The Turn of the Century

"The period from about 1898 to the World War I era has generally been regarded as one of exceptional stability and relative well-being for the American farmer," says noted economist Harold F. Williamson. This 20-year period also witnessed profound societal changes. It was during this time that a bicycle craze swept the country, even prompting John Deere to get involved with their sales. The proliferation of bicycles, and the new freedom of mobility they provided, gave impetus to improving the roads. The roads were then available to the emerging gas buggies.

The Otto-cycle (four-cycle) engine began to supplant the steam engine in providing non-animal farm power. A large crop of one-cylinder stationary "gas engines" came up in the last decade of the nineteenth century. In 1902, Hart and Parr made the first production gas tractor and became the fathers of a great industry. The automobile pioneers, Duryea, Benz, Olds, and Daimler were joined by the upstart Henry Ford. By 1900, there were 8,000 auto buggies on the American streets. But there were still 8,000,000 horses in the United States. In 1891, the Canadian implement giants Massey and

Harris had merged. In 1902, in the United States, McCormick and Deering joined, and together with several others, formed International Harvester.

## Origins of the John Deere Tractor

From approximately 1850 to 1950 the farm machinery business saw almost constant dramatic change. Each new invention spawned the next. Thus, reapers begat threshing machines, and when threshing machines required more power than could be conveniently supplied by horses, farm steam engines were developed. The portable steam engine soon became the traction engine, followed by internal combustion traction engines.

Agricultural historian R.B. Gray credits Obed Hussey with the invention of the steam engine plow in 1855. Hussey, from Baltimore, Maryland, is remembered as the inventor who first patented a reaper, much to the chagrin of Cyrus Hall McCormick. Hussey's reaper was, however, more successful than his steam plow.

Three years later, Joseph W. Fawkes of Christiana, Pennsylvania, introduced a more successful steam plowing outfit at the Illinois State Fair. It was based on a vertical boiler steam

*Previous pages*

The Model N Waterloo Boy was produced into 1924, overlapping the first two-cylinder production tractor to bear the John Deere name: the Model D. When the serial numbering system was started for the Model D, production of the Waterloo Boy was expected to die out. But instead, demand continued right along with the successful D until the Waterloo Boy serial numbers caught up with the first of those taken out for the D. Therefore, Deere officials took a block of 92 numbers out of the D sequence. The resultant numbering system is thus not easy to follow. Further complicating things, Waterloo Boy farm engines also shared the numbering system, and Waterloo Boy Model R tractors were produced simultaneously with Model Ns for a while, all on the same numbering system.

engine of 30 horsepower. It used a roller-type driving wheel 6 feet in diameter and 6 feet in length. It pulled a mounted six-bottom makeshift plow with a "power lift." Observing that the plow was the rig's weak point, John Deere made contact with Fawkes and, over the summer of 1859, developed an eight-bottom steel plow for it. In the fall of 1859, the outfit was entered in the U.S. Agricultural Contest in Chicago, where it won the gold medal. Despite this victory, the great, ungainly Fawkes engine did not prove serviceable and none were sold to the public. Nevertheless, Deere & Company had its first taste of the tractor business.

## The Waterloo Boy

By the early 1900s, giants of the industry were International Harvester, J.I. Case, and Massey-Harris, then known as the "long-line" companies. Deere, with its five lines, was not yet in their league. By 1906, International Harvester was making a gasoline traction engine. Case had been a pioneer in the steam engine business from 1892. Canadian Massey-Harris delayed entry into the tractor business until 1916. By 1918, Henry Ford was producing more Fordsons per year than the output of all the other tractor-makers combined. One might think, given its

position in the industry, that Deere would have been reluctant to step in, but that was not the case.

Deere had been successful in providing plows for neophyte tractor companies. One of the best—a 19,000-pound monster known as the "Big Four"—was made by The Gas Traction Company of Minnesota. In 1912, the Big Four appeared in the catalogs of the John Deere Plow Company with the implication that it was actually a Deere product. In fact, in a color spread, the predominant color was a green very close to that used on subsequent John Deere tractors.

The arrangement with The Gas Traction Company did not last long, but did give Deere a taste of what having its own tractor would be like. In 1912, the Deere board commissioned internal tractor experiments. The resultant machine, known as the Melvin tractor, was disappointing in field trials, however, and was dropped in 1914.

The Velie 12-24 was developed by a Deere board member, but he more or less did it on his own. The Velie tractor was used primarily by the branch houses to demonstrate Deere plows.

Up to 1914, large tractors (with weights as high as 15 tons) were the industry norm. Many farmers simply had no way to use such a monster. The directors of Deere commissioned

The difference in the drive configuration of the Model R Waterloo Boy is clearly shown here. Compared to the Model N, the drive gear is much smaller in diameter.

A Big Four tractor pulling five John Deere harvesters, circa 1912. The Big Four was big! It sported drive wheels 8 feet in diameter! A four-cylinder vertical engine of 30 horsepower provided the motivation for the 10-ton monster. In 1912, the Big Four appeared in some branch house catalogs, giving the impression that it was a Deere product, although it was not. *Deere Archives*

The Melvin tractor. Pressure from the branch houses and competition with International Harvester prompted the board of Deere & Company to commission C. H. Melvin to build an experimental tractor in 1912. It was a three-wheeled affair with three plow bottoms mounted underneath. The single (steering) wheel was behind for plowing but went first for hauling. Two seats were provided for the operator for either direction of travel. It was patterned after the 1911 Hackney, a 40-horsepower four-cylinder machine, which included a power lift for the plows. Unreliability and lack of traction caused Deere to abandon the tests and the concept. *Deere Archives*

fellow board member Joseph Dain to develop a small tractor, one that would sell for around $700. By early 1915, Dain had a prototype ready for the board to see. It was a three-wheel, all-wheel-drive machine with a four-cylinder Waukesha engine. By the end of the year, six prototypes were in the field, proving themselves to be quite successful. After a year of testing, and with a more powerful McVicker engine, it was decided to build 100 for the market.

Unfortunately, Dain died in 1917, and with him, much of the push for the tractor. While the tractor was considered a great success, and indeed it was much ahead of its time, it turned out to be too expensive. The target price of $700 had become $1,700. With the Fordson now on the market at or below the first figure, the Dain machine was no longer viable, especially since the Waterloo Gasoline Engine Company's 25-horsepower tractor—the two-cylinder Waterloo Boy—was selling for just $850. Also, the company was available for purchase.

The Waterloo Boy was a direct descendant of the first truly successful internal combustion traction engine, developed by John Froelich in 1892. Froelich mounted a single-cylinder Van Duzen engine on a Robinson steam engine running gear and devised his own drive arrangement for the wheels. With this tractor, Froelich completed a 50-day threshing run, both pulling and powering the thresher, threshing some 72,000 bushels of small grain.

Later that year, Froelich joined with others to form the Waterloo Gasoline Traction Engine Company, which would become the John Deere Tractor Company 26 years later. Four tractors of the Froelich design were built and two were sold to customers. Neither proved satisfactory, and both were returned. To generate cash flow, the company developed stationary engines, which they sold successfully. Therefore, when the company reorganized in 1895, the word "Traction" was dropped from the company's name. With the name change, Mr. Froelich also left the company. By 1906, six engine models were in production that carried the trade name "Waterloo Boy." Despite the name change, tractor experiments continued. In 1911, a man by the name of Parkhurst, from Moline, joined the Waterloo Boy Gasoline Engine Company, bringing with him three tractors of his own design, each with two-cylinder engines.

From 1911 to 1914, many variations on the theme were tried. Model designations and serial numbers from this period are rather confusing, as test articles were often rebuilt and redesignated.

Finally, in early 1914, the design of the Waterloo Boy Model R tractor was frozen; it was to be a four-wheel, rear-wheel-drive tractor with one forward speed and one reverse. The engine was a two-cylinder, four-cycle, overhead valve type, with a bore and stroke of 5.5x7 inches, giving it a displacement of 333-ci. Operating speed was 750 rpm, which produced 25 horsepower at the belt (the drawbar rating was 12).

The Model R was sold in thirteen styles, A through M, until 1918, the year Deere & Company purchased the firm. Style M, which became Model N, was introduced in 1917 and produced until 1924, when it was replaced by the first mass-production two-cylinder tractor bearing the John Deere name: the venerable Model D. (The four-cylinder Dain also bore the John Deere name, but there were only about 100 made.)

The all-wheel-drive Dain tractor, the first production tractor to bear the John Deere name. Testing and reluctance by the board delayed production until 1917. By then, Dain had died and the Waterloo Boy line was acquired.

The Velie 12-24 tractor, built and marketed by a Deere & Company board member during the time Deere was struggling to come up with a tractor of its own. Apparently Velie did not exert much pressure to have his machine taken over by Deere, but instead used it to pull and sell Deere plows. *Deere Archives*

*Below*
The Waterloo Boy Model N was introduced in 1917 and produced until 1924. It is interesting to note that, in 1920, the Model N was the first tractor to be tested by the University of Nebraska. *Author Collection*

ANY **FARM WORK** THAT CAN BE DONE BY HORSES CAN BE PERFORMED BY THIS **TRUSTY WATERLOO BOY MODEL R,** owned by Tony Ridgeway of West Unity, Ohio. The historic tractor is on display at the 1991 Two-Cylinder Days exposition at the John Deere homestead in Grand Detour, Illinois.

The Model N Waterloo Boy, the second version produced by Deere, had a two-cylinder, kerosene-burning engine that operated at 750 rpm. The N can be distinguished from the earlier Model R by the larger diameter drive gear inside the rear wheel. The Model N had two forward speeds, while the R had only one. *Author Collection*

The Waterloo Boy Model N was built between 1917 and 1924. The 465-ci two-cylinder engine produced 25 belt horsepower at 750 rpm. Some Model Ns, such as this 1920 version, had chain steering, while others had "automobile" steering. There were also several different fuel tank and radiator configurations employed. Its engine had a 6.5-inch bore and a 7-inch stroke in its final form. Earlier versions used a 5.5-inch and a 6-inch bore, although the stroke was always 7 inches. The horizontal two-cylinder engine was preceded by a horizontally opposed version and by two-cycle versions.

The pictorial logo of the Waterloo Boy tractor. The Waterloo Gasoline Engine Company was taken over by Deere & Company in 1918. Its primary product, prior to the success of the R version of the 1915 tractor, was a line of farm stationary engines. The Waterloo Boy tractor was started on gasoline but normally operated on kerosene.

# THE WATERLOO GASOLINE TRACTION ENGINE COMPANY

In 1892, John Froelich and his associates formed the Waterloo Gasoline Traction Engine Company. As founded, the company did not last long, nor were many tractors built (a total of four). Also, Mr. Froelich did not continue with the firm after it was reorganized as the Waterloo Gasoline Engine Company.

Nevertheless, the original company made a bold venture into the traction engine business. Their venture was based on a machine invented by John Froelich earlier in 1892. Froelich was driven by problems associated with farm steam power and saw the gasoline powerplant as the solution. As stated in an early sales brochure for the tractor, necessity was the mother of invention. "It was dire necessity, resulting from an unfortunate investment in the apple business on the part of our old friends Adam and Eve, that led to the invention of clothing..."

Advantages claimed for the new machine were:
1. No possibility of explosion
2. No danger of fire
3. No tank man and team necessary
4. No high-priced engineer required
5. No early firing to get up steam
6. No leaky flues
7. No broken bridges on account of weight
8. No running into obstacles as the operator is in front
9. No runaway teams on account of steam blowing off
10. No long belt to contend with

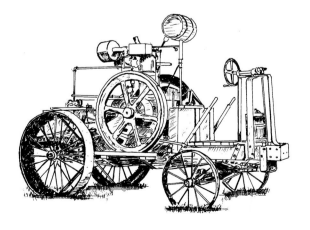

**KNOWN AS THE "GRANDPOPPA" OF ALL TWO-CYLINDER JOHN DEERE TRACTORS,** the final version of the Waterloo Boy tractor, the Model N, can be distinguished from its predecessors by the size of the large drive gears attached to the rear wheels. The Model N was the first mass-produced tractor, with 20,000 machines manufactured during its production run.

# Chapter Two

# MAKING TRACTORS IN THE TWENTIES

## Competing with Steam

"If it hadn't been for the free publicity given by our friends, the enemy, I really don't know if we should have pulled through." These are the words of Charles Hart, of the Hart-Parr Company, when he saw the laughing scorn of the steam engine salesmen turned back on them as the gas engine gained ground. Their derision was apparently along the lines of the Shakespearean quotation, "Methinks you protest too much."

By 1910, there was approximately 28 million total farm horsepower—animal and mechanical—in the United States. Of this, about 15 percent was provided by steam and about 8 percent by internal combustion. Steam power was a maturing technology, finding routine use in ships and on railroads. With few exceptions, the internal combustion (gas) engines used for farm power were of the four-cycle type, with automatic intake valves and hit-miss governors and low-voltage, battery-powered ignition. The first gas tractors were basically steam engine chassis with a gas engine mounted. There were 600 of them operating in 1910. The next 20 years would see almost a million more in use.

Rumely, Hart-Parr, and International Harvester were the big gas tractor producers during these years. Hart-Parr sent three and Rumely sent two trainloads of their gas tractors to the emerging wheat lands of Western Canada in 1912.

Rumely was also a steam engine maker, as were Case and Minneapolis. At the turn of the century, the steamer was so reliable and steady in its power, compared to the gas tractor, that many farmers held the gas tractor in derision. Especially in the Canadian prairies, the big steamers were winning converts to power farming. Records, such as 160 acres plowed in 24 hours (with a 40-horsepower Reeves), were made. At the 1909 Manitoba Fair, a 25-horsepower Garr-Scott steam traction engine recorded a plowing rate of one acre in 7 minutes, 58 seconds.

Nevertheless, with more and better gas tractors coming into the field, the tide began to turn. In 1908, the Winnipeg Industrial Exhibition began sponsoring comparative tractor trials. Now the public could witness and compare the performance of various steam and gas tractors. The obvious convenience and versatility of the gas tractor became apparent. Yet, as late as 1920, there were still 15 brands of steam tractors available, and in that year they produced 1,766 machines.

Deere management watched the unfolding tractor events with detachment. They were in the plow business and were selling plows of all sizes and types to go with the new tractors, both steam and gas.

In 1900, Deere's competitors were The Oliver Chilled Plow Company in the United States and Cockshutt in Canada. After the 1902 formation of International Harvester (IH), Deere management became concerned. Their concern was not about product competition, but about IH winning the hearts and minds of the independent dealers. If this happened, it would either force Deere out of business or force them under Harvester's control. William Butterworth was probably more concerned by the later prospect.

Butterworth led the Deere board of directors toward a policy of aggressive defense. To prevent being swallowed up by IH, they would have to become too large a bite. Yet, the tractor part of the business still presented a quandary. The management of Deere struggled with the question of whether to enter the tractor market or to continue to tailor their implements to the tractors of others. To enter would alienate some of their best customers; not to enter would leave Harvester with a big advantage.

## Competing with International Harvester

Following the Harvester merger in 1902, Deere & Company at first took a hands-off, self-effacing stance, emphasizing to dealers and farmers that the two companies' product lines didn't compete. International Harvester made harvesters and mowers and the like; Deere made plows and cultivators. Many independent dealers sold both lines of implements. In fact, many of Deere's branch houses had been handling non-competing lines of wagons and haymaking tools, planters, and spreaders.

By 1906, however, IH took a more aggressive competitive posture by encouraging exclusivity of its product lines at the dealers. Harvester also began to market farm wagons, gas engines, and manure spreaders by buying the companies that made them, sometimes surreptitiously. To defend itself from further monopolization of the marketplace by International Harvester, Deere made its first acquisition of another company: the Fort Smith Wagon Company. This acquisition was made just before the death of Charles Deere in 1907. Later that year, the John Deere Plow Co., Ltd., was formed in Canada.

Finally, on January 6, 1910, the Deere directors issued a decision on reorganizing the company into a more consolidated entity. The same written decision included the statement that Deere & Company would enter the harvester business.

In 1911, Deere entered upon an aggressive policy of acquisition. Companies were added that made shellers, elevators, spreaders, and haymaking equipment. Some of these companies were moved to the Moline area. In 1912, ground was broken in East Moline for a new harvester plant. Now the cat was out of the bag—Deere had taken on International Harvester head-on. It was almost a foregone conclusion that tractors would be next, as International Harvester was by then the number one tractor maker in the world.

It's hard to believe, now that the words "John Deere" are almost synonymous with "farm tractor," that it was such a struggle for the company to get into the tractor business. But, following Deere's purchase of the Waterloo Boy in 1918, the company found the "Boy" to be an immediate success, and it continued to be successful during the years of World War I. Over 4,000 Waterloo Boys were exported to England to aid in

A John Deere GP tractor with a check-row corn planter. The spool of wire, mounted to the left side of the tractor, is pulled out as the tractor proceeds across the field; evenly-spaced knots in the wire trip the planter. Check-row planting allowed cultivating both ways. *Author Collection*

overcoming food shortages. English tractors used the brand name "Overtime" rather than Waterloo Boy.

Prosperity continued for a time after the November 11, 1918, Armistice. Deere sold more than 5,000 Waterloo Boys in 1920. But Henry Ford had begun producing Fordsons in earnest in 1918. His 1920 production was 67,000! Ford's production not only exceeded that of International Harvester, it exceeded that of all other tractor makers combined.

### The Fordson Phenomenon

What was a Fordson? Anyone over 70 years old who lived in farming country knows! For those who don't, the Fordson was a new concept in farm tractors, mass-produced by the Model T car king. It was a 2,700-pound tractor of 20 belt horsepower and 10 on the drawbar. Henry's only son, Edsel, was at an age where he wanted to become active in the business, so a new tractor company was opened as "Henry Ford and Son." The tractor was named the "Fordson" for short.

In most respects, the Fordson was a worthy tractor for its price; about two-thirds that of the Waterloo Boy. The Fordson's light weight and poor balance, however, limited its traction and allowed rearing problems, where it was prone to tipping over backwards. It used a flywheel magneto, similar to that used on the Model T car. When this worked, it worked well. When it was "off," the farmer with only a Sunday school vocabulary was at a severe disadvantage.

### Enter the All-purpose Tractor

In 1921, a severe economic downturn surprised almost everyone. The agricultural industry was especially hard hit. Henry Ford knew what to do—he first cut the $785 price to $620. Other tractor makers followed suit, including Deere (dropping the Waterloo Boy price to $890). So the irrepressible Ford further cut his price to $395. Only International Harvester had the strength to counterattack.

The competition that the Fordson stirred up provided the incentive to develop a machine that could do what the Fordson could not. The Fordson was not useful for the cultivation of crops. It did not have a driveshaft power take-off, and therefore was not suitable for the new harvester implements. Most of all, while it could replace some of the horses on a farm, it could not replace them all.

In July 1921, when the Fordson threatened the whole International Harvester empire, General Manager Alexander Legge called in his engineers and asked them what had happened to the "motor cultivator" designs they'd been working on. Head of the Experimental Department, Edward Johnston reported that his team had focused on one design, which they called the "Farmall." Johnston insisted the Farmall could beat the Fordson in every respect. When told this, Legge immediately ordered the construction of 20 more hand-built examples. He also ordered a full compliment of implements to be customized for the Farmall, all to be ready for testing in 1922.

In 1924, some 200 production models were sold to customers. Harvester field men watched closely as the farmers put the new Farmall through its paces under actual conditions. By 1926, the new Rock Island (Illinois) plant was in operation and Farmalls were rolling out the door.

Deere's first reaction to the Fordson was to take a look at the Waterloo Boy in comparison to other tractors in the field. International Harvester had introduced a new 15-30 in 1921 and a 10-20 in 1922. Hart-Parr had come out with a new 12-25 and a 15-30 in 1918. All looked much more like a Fordson than like a Waterloo Boy. All were smaller, lighter, had automotive-type

steering and had the radiator/fan in front and an engine hood like a car. Even before Deere's acquisition, Waterloo Boy engineers were working on a modernized version built after the fashion of the competition. Deere engineers quickly picked up on it and developed it into the first production two-cylinder tractor to be called a John Deere: the Model D. To say that the Model D was a success would be an understatement. Its 30-year production run is the longest of any tractor to date and firmly established Deere as a maker of quality tractors.

## The Advent of the GP

The Farmall differed radically from all other tractors. Its small front wheels were close together in order to run between two rows. Its rear axle did not run straight between the rear wheel hubs but was connected down to the hubs through a large gear mesh. The result of this arrangement was a tractor with its rear axle built high, providing 30 inches of clearance above the ground. The larger-than-normal-diameter rear wheels were wide enough apart to straddle the two rows that the front wheels ran between.  It had a 20-horsepower engine and weighed about 4,000 pounds. Its main implement was a two-row cultivator mounted to the front frame. This made power cultivation of crops, such as corn and cotton, practical for the first time with a volume production tractor.

The new Farmall did not replace the standard tractor; the production of these continued to increase. By 1928, however, the Fordson's annual production was down to 12,500 and Henry Ford gave up, saying he needed the production space for his new Model A car. At International Harvester, the combination of standard tread tractors and the new Farmall gave the company a 70 percent share of the tractor market after the Fordson was gone. Deere & Company knew it had to react to Harvester's dominance of the field.

In response to the Farmall, John Deere brought out the 10-horsepower (at the drawbar) Model GP ("General Purpose"), the second production tractor to bear the John Deere name. The belt rating was 20 horsepower. The GP was introduced in 1928. It had the same basic layout as the Model D, with widespread front wheels. The GP, however, had a high arched front axle that enabled it to straddle the center row and thereby cultivate not two rows as the Farmall, but three rows at one time. A three-row planter was also developed. The GP was rated for a two-bottom plow.

The GP featured a mechanical implement power lift system, which was an industry first, plus individual rear wheel brakes. It also incorporated a 520-rpm power take-off. Like the Model D, and indeed all John Deere tractors until 1960, it used a two-cylinder engine similar to that of the Waterloo Boy. The GP's engine began life with 312 ci, but after 1931, displacement was increased to 339 ci. The GP engine was of the L-head type and engine speed was 950 rpm. A three-speed transmission was used. The basic weight of the Model GP was 3,600 pounds.

Although the GP continued in the line until 1935, its acceptance by farmers, especially in the South, and its performance in the field, was disappointing. Acceptance was low primarily because of the three-row concept. Farmers wanted two-row equipment in some areas and four-row in others. Additionally, the $800 price tag was high for a 10/20-horsepower

The box-like affair over the radiator of this John Deere Model C contained the radiator shutters. With the "thermocycle" (gravity) water circulation system, the use of a thermostat was not possible. Thus, to regulate coolant temperature, the operator hand-adjusted the shutters. With kerosene fuels, it was important to keep the temperature as high as possible without boiling.

*Opposite*
This Model C, like the subsequent Model GP, used an unusual post-type seat support. The C was an "experimental" forerunner of the GP. The designation was changed primarily to better counter the new McCormick-Deering Farmall and Oliver Hart-Parr general-purpose tractors that were ravishing the marketplace in the late 1920s. The second reason for the change was due to the quality of the telephone system of the time. It was difficult to distinguish "Model C" from "Model D" over the phone.

tractor, with the Farmall selling for around $600. The GP should have had more horsepower, but Deere engineers could not get the engine to come up to expectations until 1931, when the bore was increased a quarter of an inch. The rating was then upped to 16/24 horsepower.

The John Deere Model GP actually began life as the Model C in 1927, when 25 were built. Sixteen of these were rebuilt into an improved configuration. Sixty-nine more of this new configuration were also built, but more problems were encountered, so 37 of these were recalled and modified. After 110 Model Cs were built, the designation was changed to GP to better counter the "general purpose" image of the Farmall, and because "C" sounded too much like the designation of their other tractor, the D. (One must remember the quality of the telephone system of the late twenties.) The names "Powerfarmer" and "Farmrite" were considered but discarded.

During the experiments associated with the Model C, one configuration was tried that used a tricycle layout; that is, two front wheels close together and rear wheels on a 50-inch tread. As soon as it was recognized that the three-row concept of the standard GP was not being accepted in all quarters, this tricycle GP was brought out. About 23 were interspersed in the GP production during late 1929 and early 1930. Two of these had special rear treads of 68 inches to accommodate two standard potato rows.

Later in 1929, the GPWT, or GP Wide-Tread, was introduced. It had longer axles, giving it a 76-inch rear tread and allowing it to straddle two regular rows. In addition, some 203 were built with the special potato-row axles. In 1931, dished wheels were developed, allowing the standard Wide-Tread to be converted for potato rows and the "P" (potato) series of GPs was eliminated.

One place in which the Farmall still held the advantage was in operator vision for cultivating. Therefore, in 1932, the hood of the GPWT was narrowed and the steering changed so that the shaft ran over the engine like the Farmall, rather than alongside the engine as on the other GPs.

The first John Deere orchard tractor was based on the GP. It had fender skirts covering the rear wheels down to below the hubs and extending over the flywheel and belt pulley. This model, the GPO, came out in 1930. Some of these were purchased by the Lindeman Company and were fitted with crawler tracks for use in the large hilly apple orchards around Yakima, Washington.

Over 30,500 GPs were sold by the end of production in 1935.

Although at first glance this looks like a John Deere GP, it is actually a Model C, the forerunner of the GP. This example, serial number 200109, is owned by the Kellers of Forest Junction, Wisconsin. The Kellers—father Walter, son Bruce, and grandson Jason—own over 160 collectible tractors.

KELLER'S BEAUTIFULLY RESTORED MODEL C, **THE FORERUNNER OF THE JOHN DEERE GP TRACTORS.** Many Model Cs were recalled in 1928, **MAKING THIS LOVELY SPECIMEN RARE INDEED.**

**INCREASED VERSATILITY. THAT'S HOW THE JOHN DEERE MODEL GP WAS MARKETED TO FARMERS** rather than as a replacement for the Model D. Notice the different type of seat mounting on Keller's rare side-steer tricycle 1929 GP, serial number 204213.

# JOHN DEERE MODEL GP

**General Specifications: Wide-Front Version**
**Years Produced: 1928–1935**
**First Serial Number: 200211**
**Last Serial Number: 230745**
**Total Built: 30,534 (approx.), all types**
**Price, New: $800 (1928): $1,200 (1931)**

| Horsepower (Max.) | Drawbar | PTO/Belt |
|---|---|---|
| 5.75x6.0 | 18.7 | 24.7 |
| 6.0x6.0 | 26.2 | 29.6 |

**Engine Displacement**
  5.75x6.0 Engine (to S/N 223802): 312ci
  6.0x6.0 Engine (to S/N 223803): 339ci

**Engine Rated rpm: 950**

**Wheels, Standard**
  **Rear: 42x10**
  **Front: 24x6**

**Length: 112 inches**
**Height to Radiator: 56 inches**
**Weight: 3,600 pounds**

**Transmission**
  **Speeds Forward: 3**

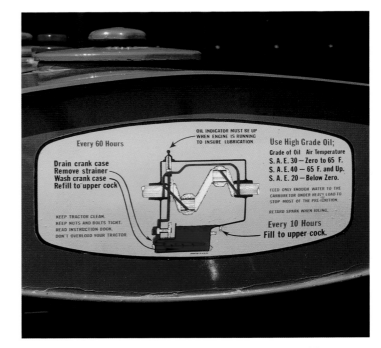

Lubrication requirements were visually augmented by this diagram that graced the end of the fuel tank on most of the older John Deere models. It was right in front of the driver where it couldn't be missed.

Many felt that Deere had finally gotten it right with the "over-the-top" steer GPWT. It was most like the successful Farmall and Oliver all-purpose machines.

During experiments with the John Deere Model C, the forerunner of the Model GP, one configuration tried was the tricycle layout. Later, when it was determined that the regular GP's arched wide-front axle and its attendant three-row equipment were not accepted in some areas, a tricycle version of the GP was brought out. About 23 of these were made in 1929 and 1930. The one shown, owned by the Kellers of Forest Junction, Wisconsin, is probably the only one that was not later returned to the factory to be modified into the GPWT (general-purpose, Wide-Tread) configuration and renumbered with a 400000-series serial number.

## KELLER'S LOVELY GPWT TRACTOR

(General-Purpose, Wide-Tread) features innovative over-the-top steering. Previous versions of the tricycle GP had an angled steering shaft.

Chapter Three

# A NEW DEAL
## FOR FARMERS

## John Deere Models A and B

By 1929, there were seven major long-line implement companies vying for the business. They were ranked as follows:

- International Harvester     52 percent
- Deere & Company     21 percent
- J.I. Case     8 percent
- Oliver Farm Equipment     8 percent
- Minneapolis-Moline     4 percent
- Massey-Harris     4 percent
- Allis-Chalmers     3 percent

Interestingly, each one of these companies was engaged in a search for the perfect all-purpose tractor.

After the tractor price war, business had been quite good for the implement makers, although Charles Deere Wiman still worried about Harvester's dominance. However, it wasn't Harvester that was the unseen threat in the summer of 1929, but the twin specters of economic depression and drought. The market crash in October did not, at first, affect Deere or the other long-line companies. By the summer of 1930, however, layoffs and factory closings were happening at Deere as well as the others. Still, no one seemed to appreciate the catastrophe that was developing.

Overall industrial output was cut in half by 1933; unemployment soared. Prices, especially farm prices, plummeted. To add to this misery, severe droughts occurred in 1930 and 1934. Winds swept away the topsoil from Kansas and Oklahoma. To make matters worse for Deere, management had just adopted a policy of financing farmers' purchases of Deere equipment. Now, the farmers who could were concentrating on subsistence farming; they had no cash to pay off equipment loans. Deere was in the ticklish spot of alienating (or bankrupting) its customers if it forced collection.

It was within this forgoing scene that Deere President Charles Wiman made a fateful decision. He instructed Theo Brown, the research manager, to aggressively pursue the development of two new general-purpose tractors. There was to be a two-plow and a one-plow version. The idea was to replace the disappointing GP and to counter the successful Farmall and Oliver row-crop tractors. Although Wiman was forced to eliminate some non-machinery research and to even close some experimental farms, it was his conviction that power farming was the wave of the future. It was his appreciation for machinery and his engineering training and interest that spurred the tractor program.

## Development of the Models A and B

In the depths of the Great Depression, Charles Wiman bet the company on the two new general-purpose tractors. The Model A came out first in April 1934, the B almost a year later in 1935. There were at least eight experimental tractors built before settling on the configuration of the A. Six of these incorporated a new four-speed transmission. The other two used the traditional three-speed unit. These tractors were known respectively as Models AA-1 and AA-3. After thorough testing, the AA-1 configuration became the Model A. The Model B was essentially a two-thirds scale model of the A, incorporating all the same features.

By 1935, the power and weight of the GP were exceeding that of the new Model A. A new smaller, more agile tractor was needed to compete with a team of horses. The Model B filled the niche not only because of its smaller size but also because it cost less and used less fuel than larger tractors, including the GP. Nebraska Tractor Test Number 2232 showed the B producing a little over 10 horsepower hours per gallon of low-cost kerosene—an improvement of about 1 horsepower hour per gallon over the GP.

In 1932, when Brown and his team began working on the new tractors, the general-purpose, or row-crop, tractor had come into its own. By then, however, it was clear that there was a market for both row-crop tractors and standard tread tractors. Therefore, standard tread, or "regular," versions of both the A and B were introduced as the AR and BR. These were not considered to be general-purpose tractors as they did not incorporate the implement lift, adjustable wheel tread, or differential steering brakes. Orchard versions, the AO and BO, were also available. The Lindeman Company of Yakima, Washington, converted some 2,000 BO models to its Lindeman Crawler by adding crawler tracks. Industrial wheel tractor versions of both the A and B tractors were also available as the AI and BI.

The tricycle configuration developed into the conventional arrangement for general-purpose machines with the two front wheels close together. By 1937, variations with one front wheel, with adjustable wide fronts, and extra high-clearance (hi-crop) versions of all front-end types were made available.

The Model A was introduced first simply because of the limitations of manpower and facilities. The Model B was originally available with pneumatic tires (the A was not), and, like the A, it also had a four-speed transmission, a PTO, and belt pulley. Its engine, a scaled version of that in the A, had enough power for one 16-inch plow (the A was capable of pulling two 14s).

What made the Models A and B so special? After all, the Farmall had been out for 10 years by the time the A was introduced. These two new GPs had two remarkable features that were industry firsts: fully adjustable rear wheel widths on splined axles and hydraulic implement lifts. These alone were enough to ensure the success of the A and B. In addition, the one-piece rear axle housing provided more crop clearance and allowed a center location for attachment of the drawbar, as well as a center location for the PTO.

Production of the Model As and Bs continued through 1952. Almost 300,000 Model As were built, and more than 300,000 Model Bs. These tractors were immensely profitable for both Deere and the farmers who bought them. Over the years, there was a continual process of upgrade and improvement.

*Previous pages*
This rare ANH is owned by the Kellers of Forest Junction, Wisconsin. The 1938 model has a four-speed transmission and a 309-ci engine.

*Opposite*
One of several variations on the logo theme that graced the early John Deere tractors. This one is on Model B serial number 1000.

One great line of demarcation occurred in 1938, however, when styling came to the John Deere tractor.

In other industrial areas, pleasing aesthetic proportions were in vogue, from trucks to telephones, and some well-known designers were achieving a measure of prominence. One of these was Henry Dreyfuss of New York City. Charles Stone, who headed Deere's manufacturing, was approached by his engineers to allow them to contact Dreyfuss about tractor styling. Stone was reluctantly acquiescent.

Dreyfuss made a deal with the Deere officials and within a month had a wooden mockup of a new version of the Model B ready for review. The functional beauty of it startled the Deere engineers. This was much more than a radiator grille addition. The styling was indeed functional. The striking new hood was slimmer, enhancing cultivator visibility, and the new radiator cover, more than just a grille, protected the cooling system from collecting debris.

In an incredibly short time, the Deere-Dreyfuss team brought both the A and B styled models out for the l938 season. The acceptance by the customers led to a continuing styling improvement program.

International Harvester was not caught napping by the competition. Seeing the trend toward more functional and eye-pleasing designs, Harvester engaged the services of Raymond Lowey, another noted industrial designer (who later gained worldwide renown with his rakish design of the 1953 Studebaker car line). Lowey was commissioned to overhaul the entire IH product line, from the company logo to product operator ergonomics. By late 1938, the same year that John Deere brought out "styled" tractors, Harvester introduced the new TD-18 crawler tractor. The rest of the line followed a year later.

Under its skin, the Model A remained much the same after styling for three years. For the B, however, engine displacement was increased from 149 to 175 ci at this time. In 1941, the A received a displacement increase from 309 to 321 ci, and the transmissions of both models went from four speeds to six. This transmission change was first accomplished by employing a three-speed gearbox and a high-low range auxiliary. Two shift levers were used. Later, a single-lever arrangement was substituted.

The Model A finished its career with this engine/transmission combination, but the B enjoyed one more displacement increase in 1947 to 190 ci. Along with this change, both models went from a channel-iron frame to a pressed-steel frame. The 1947 to 1952 Models A and B are known as "late-styled" versions.

## The Models G and H

As the decade of the thirties ended, the more progressive farmers generally had outgrown their horses. Now they were in the market for tractors that would handle larger implements, move them faster, and further multiply the efforts of manpower. They also saw the need for a small tractor to replace one and two horses for small jobs.

Perfect restoration, as is only befitting such a rare collector's item as this 1938 ANH. Only 26 were made!

# JOHN DEERE MODEL A

**General Specifications: Row-Crop Version**
**Years Produced: 1934–1952**
**First Serial Number: 410008**
**Last Serial Number: 703384**
**Total Built: 300,000 (approx.), all types**
**Price, New: $2,400 (1952)**

| Horsepower (Max.) | Drawbar | PTO/Belt |
|---|---|---|
| 5.5x6.5 | 18.7 | 24.7 |
| 5.5x6.75(kero) | 26.2 | 29.6 |
| 5.5x6.75(gas) | 34.1 | 38.0 |

**Engine Displacement**
5.75x6.5 Engine (to S/N 498999): 309ci
5.5x5.75 Engine (to S/N 499000): 321ci

**Engine Rated rpm: 975**

**Wheels/Tires, Standard**

| | Wheels | Tires |
|---|---|---|
| Rear | 50x6 inches | 11.0x38 |
| Front | 24x4 inches | 5.5x16 |

**Unstyled**

| | |
|---|---|
| Length | 112 inches |
| Height to Radiator | 56.0 inches |
| Weight | 3,525 pounds |

**1938–1947**

| | |
|---|---|
| Length | 133.0 inches |
| Height to Radiator | 62.5 inches |
| Weight | 3,783 pounds |

**1947–1952**

| | |
|---|---|
| Length | 134.0 inches |
| Height to Radiator | 63.9 inches |
| Weight | 4,909 pounds |

**Transmission**
Speeds Forward(early): 4
(after S/N 499000): 6

The Wico magneto on an early unstyled Model A.

The Model B was introduced in 1935 as a smaller version of Deere's great Model A. This 1935 version of the Model B was rated at only 9.28 drawbar horsepower at the University of Nebraska tests. The last B, the 1952 model, was rated at 24.46 drawbar horsepower, showing how the model grew during its life.

## JOHN DEERE MODEL B

**General Specifications: Row-Crop Version**
**Years Produced: 1935–1952**
**First Serial Number: 1000**
**Last Serial Number: 310775**
**Total Built: 300,000 (approx.), all types**
**Price, New: $1,900 (1952)**

| Horsepower (Max.) | Drawbar | PTO/Belt |
|---|---|---|
| 4.25x5.25 | 11.8 | 16.0 |
| 4.5x5.50 | 14.0 | 18.5 |
| 4.6x5.50(gas) | 24.6 | 27.6 |
| (dist.) | 21.1 | 23.5 |

**Engine Displacement**
4.25x5.25 Engine (to S/N 59999): 149ci
4.50x5.50 Engine (to S/N 200999): 175ci
4.69x5.50 Engine (to S/N 310775): 190ci

**Engine Rated rpm**
(S/N 200999): 1,150
(S/N 310775): 1,250

**Wheels/Tires, Standard**

| | Wheels | Tires |
|---|---|---|
| Rear | 48x5.25 | 10.0x38 |
| Front | 22x3.25 | 5.5x16 |

**Unstyled**
| | |
|---|---|
| Length | 120.5 inches |
| Height to Radiator | 56.0 inches |
| Weight | 2,760 pounds |

**1938–1947**
| | |
|---|---|
| Length | 125.5 inches |
| Height to Radiator | 57.0 inches |
| Weight | 2,880 pounds |

**1947–1952**
| | |
|---|---|
| Length | 132.3 inches |
| Height to Radiator | 59.6 inches |
| Weight | 4,000 pounds |

**Transmission**
Speeds Forward: 4

The arrival of the big John Deere Model G in 1938 was appreciated by the larger-acreage farmers who needed at least some row-crop capabilities. The G was virtually the power equivalent of the D. The advent of the Model H in 1939 was welcomed by the small-acreage farmers; it was the power equivalent of the original Model B. Both were available as row-crops only.

Not long after the G's introduction, Deere began receiving complaints about overheating, especially from farmers in warmer climates. Deere concluded that the original radiator was too small. Accordingly, at Serial Number 4,251, the height of the radiator was increased. Those with earlier serial numbers are now known as "low-radiator Gs."

The G was one of the last John Deere tractors to receive Dreyfuss styling, in 1942. At the same time, its transmission was upgraded to six speeds and it was reidentified as the GM (for "modernized") in order to get a price increase past the War Price Board. After the end of World War II, it again reverted to either G, or New G.

The unstyled and GM versions of the tractor were available only as dual-front tricycle types. Postwar versions were also available in single-front-wheel, wide-front, and hi-crop arrangements.

The H was unique among the GP tractors, in that the power was taken off the camshaft rather than the crankshaft. This was done for a number of reasons, all relating to the fact that the H engine was rated at 1,400 rpm and could (with governor override) be operated at 1,800 rpm. By taking the power out through the camshaft, a 2:1 reduction had taken place and the speed was cut in half. This meant a simpler transmission and the elimination of bull gears normally used on the rear axles.

There were four versions of the H:
• Model H: Dual narrow front, row-crop
• Model HN: Same as the H, but with a single front wheel
• Model HWH: Same as the H, but with 8-38 rear tires and an adjustable hi-crop front axle
• Model HNH: The same as the HWH, but with a single front wheel

*Opposite*
The John Deere B was essentially a scale model of the A, although there are subtle differences between the two in design details. The steering post and gear set shown here are on a 1935 B. It is somewhat different from the Model A post.

ONE OF SEVERAL "FIRST EDITIONS" OWNED BY THE KELLERS, **THIS JEWEL IS THE VERY FIRST JOHN DEERE MODEL B TRACTOR**, serial number 1000. First-year Model Bs are referred to as "Brass Tags," named for their brass serial number plates.

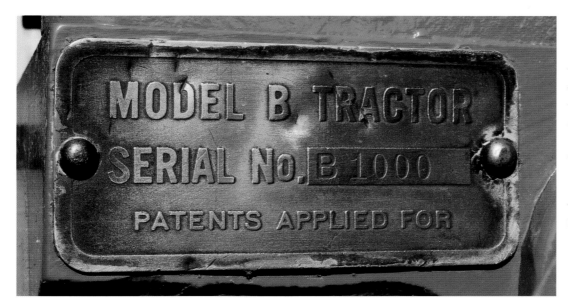

This brass tag is what every tractor collector dreams of finding on a relic behind someone's barn: the tag indicates this is the first of over 300,000 John Deere Model B tractors. It is, however, like most valuable antique tractors, already found. It belongs to the Kellers of Forest Junction, Wisconsin.

Although outwardly remaining much the same over the years, the Model B engine grew in displacement from 149 ci to 190 ci over its lifetime. The engine shown is on B serial number 1000, the very first Model B.

*Opposite*
A 1936 "short-hood" Model B, serial number 18378, owned and restored by Lyle Pals of Egan, Illinois. Pals bought it from a neighbor who bought it new. Until serial number 42133, the Model B's frame was 5 inches shorter. After a gap in the numbering sequence to 42199 and beginning with serial number 42200, Bs are known as "long-hoods" or "long-frames."

THE JOHN DEERE MODEL B WAS **THE BEST-SELLING TWO-CYLINDER JOHN DEERE TRACTOR EVER PRODUCED.** OVER 306,000 TRACTORS WERE SOLD! This restored 1936 model has been owned by the family of Lyle Pals of Egan, Illinois, since he was a boy.

IN ALMOST EVERY RESPECT, THE EARLY MODEL BS WERE SIMPLY SMALLER VERSIONS OF THE JOHN DEERE MODEL A. This beautiful Model B sports a ring-type drawbar of the type used in the 1934–1936 timeframe.

**ONE OF ONLY 50!** THIS IMPECCABLE
1938 JOHN DEERE BWH (wide wheel spacing,
high-crop clearance), serial number 57718,
is the favorite of owner Bruce Keller, Forest Junction,
Wisconsin. THE KELLER FAMILY HAS ONE OF THE
TOP-FIVE **ANTIQUE TRACTOR COLLECTIONS
IN THE WORLD.**

The 1938 John Deere BWH. The tractor saved the company from the overwhelming onslaught of the Fordson, which could not cultivate and had no PTO.

In its element, this rare John Deere BWH straddles three rows of late June corn. It will be several more weeks before the corn is tall enough to touch the front axle. The BWH has longer kingpin struts and larger rear tires than a BW.

The 1938 John Deere BWH was specially configured for corn, sugar cane, and cotton cultivation. STILL TRYING TO BE SURE THEY GOT THEIR SHARE OF THE ALL-PURPOSE TRACTOR TRADE, JOHN DEERE EMBLAZONED THE HOODS OF THE NEW MODELS A AND B WITH THE WORDS "GENERAL PURPOSE."

The carburetor of Lyle Pals'
1949 AWH.

*Opposite*
Most available mufflers for
John Deere As are too tall to
be correct. Lyle Pals disas-
sembles mufflers such as this
one, cuts off the excess, and
welds them back together.
Such are the lengths restorers
will go to achieve originality.

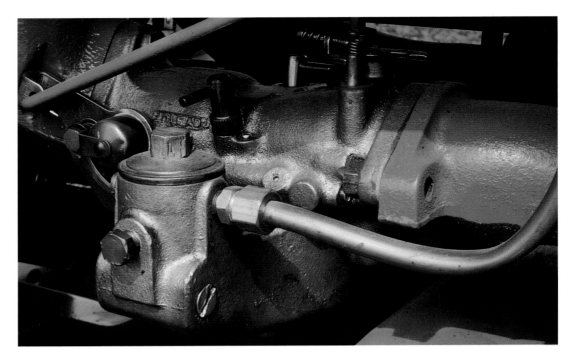

This late-styled Model AWH uses 12.4x42 rear tires.

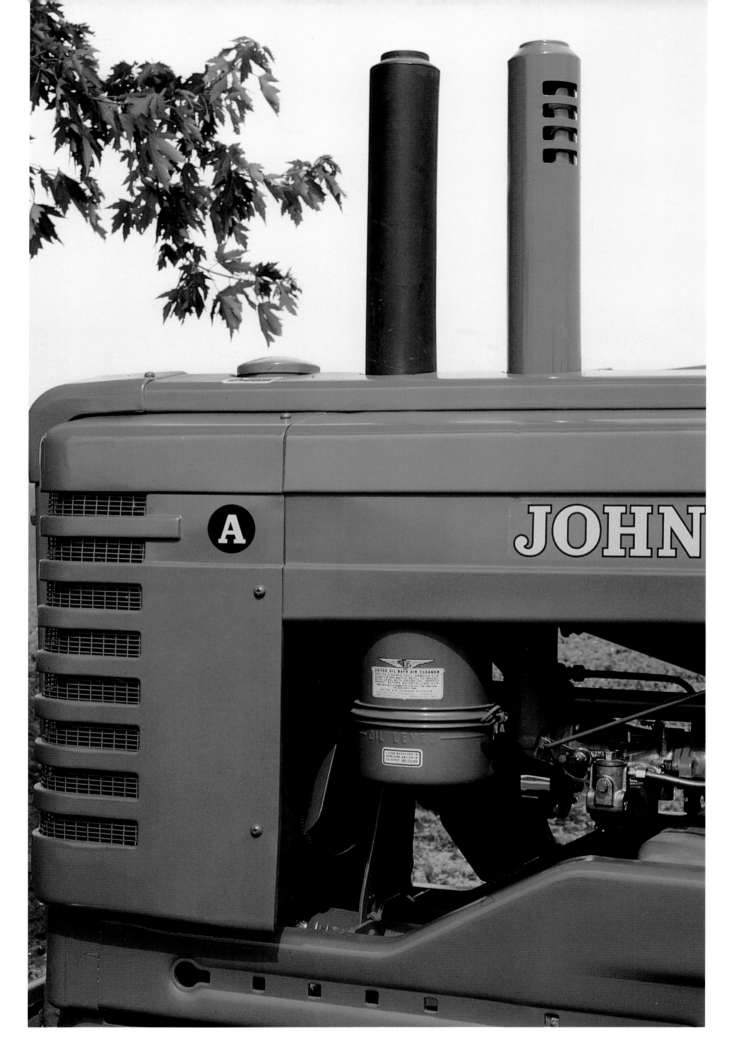

**THIS EXTREMELY RARE JOHN DEERE MODEL AOS** is displayed in the Haese Memorial Village, Forest Junction, Wisconsin. **THE AOS DESIGNATION WAS GIVEN TO DIFFERENTIATE BETWEEN IT AND THE PREVIOUS ORCHARD VERSION OF THE MODEL A,** the AO, which did not incorporate the flowing sheet metal to allow the tractor to slip through without snagging or damaging the trees.

Author Robert N. Pripps with his 1948 late-styled Model B. The tractor was restored in 1992. The scene is the author's maple forest in north-central Wisconsin.

The cows seem awed by the horsepower of this 1951 Styled G. Note the bulge in the frame side rails to make room for the G's 412.5-ci engine. The ruggedness of the G, plus the size of its engine, makes it a favorite with the antique tractor pull hobbyist. Some reportedly get as much as 100 horsepower from the modified two-cylinder engine. The G shown is owned by Lyle Pals of Egan, Illinois.

There were three designations for the Model 320. The first 2,566 carried only the 320 designation. After this, the production was divided between the 320S version, such as the one shown, and a version with a lower stance designated the 320U. The original 320s were configured like the later 320S.

LYLE PALS' RARE 1952 LATE-STYLED
MODEL BWH, SERIAL NUMBER 289887.
**CLAM FENDERS AND
LIGHTS** ARE AMONG SOME OF
THE BEST FEATURES OF THESE MODELS.
When Deere decided to cut the BWH
from the model line, it made these features
standard equipment on future Model BWs.

## JOHN DEERE MODEL G

**General Specifications**
**Years Produced:** 1938–1953
**First Serial Number:** 1000
**Last Serial Number:** 64530
**Total Built:** 64,000 (approx.), all types
**Price, New:** $2,600 (1953)

| Horsepower (Max.) | Drawbar | PTO/Belt |
|---|---|---|
| | 34.5 | 38.1 |

**Engine Displacement**
6.12x7.0 Engine: 412.5ci

**Engine Rated rpm:** 975

**Wheels/Tires, Standard**

| | Wheels | Tires |
|---|---|---|
| Rear | 51.5x7 inches | 12.0x38 |
| Front | 24x inches | 6.0x16 |

**Unstyled**
| | |
|---|---|
| Length | 135.0 inches |
| Height to Radiator | 61.5 inches |
| Weight | 4,400 pounds |

**GM**
| | |
|---|---|
| Length | 137.5 inches |
| Height to Radiator | 65.9 inches |
| Weight | 5,624 pounds |

**New G**
| | |
|---|---|
| Length | 137.5 inches |
| Height to Radiator | 65.9 inches |
| Weight | 5,624 pounds |

**Transmission**
Speeds Forward (early): 4
(after S/N 13000): 6

## JOHN DEERE MODEL H

**General Specifications**
**Years Produced:** 1939–1947
**First Serial Number:** 1000
**Last Serial Number:** 61116
**Total Built:** 60,000 appr., all types
**Price, New:** $650 (1940)

| Horsepower (Max.) | Drawbar | PTO/Belt |
|---|---|---|
| | 12.5 | 14.8 |

**Engine Displacement:** 99.7ci

**Engine Bore and Stroke:** 3.56x5.0 inches

**Engine Rated rpm:** 1,400

| | Tires |
|---|---|
| Rear | 8x32 |
| Front | 4x15 |

| | |
|---|---|
| Length | 111.3 inches |
| Height to Radiator | 52 inches |
| Weight | 3035 pounds |

**Transmission**
Speeds Forward: 3

Wife object to your tractor collection? Jim Kenney of Streater, Illinois, solved the problem by getting wife Nancy one of her own. Nancy is shown here on her beautifully restored John Deere H.
*Author Collection*

# NOTHING SOUNDS QUITE AS SWEET AS A JOHN DEERE ANTIQUE.

Beautiful and functional, this late-styled John Deere Model B row crop has a mounted cordwood saw.

TODAY, MANY COLLECTORS GO SO FAR AS TO ACQUIRE 20 OR 30 ACRES TO PLANT, CULTIVATE, AND HARVEST WITH THEIR ANTIQUE MACHINERY. *Author Collection*

# Chapter Four

# POST-WAR CHANGES

## Enter the Utility Tractor

"You haven't got enough money to buy my patents," Harry Ferguson bluntly told Henry Ford, probably the richest man in the world in 1938.

"Well, you need me as much as I need you," responded Ford, "so what do you suggest?"

Ferguson's proposal was that Ford should build tractors incorporating Ferguson's patented hydraulic lift system. And he, Ferguson, would build implements for it and a dealer organization to sell and service it. With a handshake, the world's first "utility tractor" was launched. The result was the famous Ford-Ferguson 9N.

Just what is a utility tractor? The definition has changed somewhat over the years as tractors have changed. The first mention of such in R.B. Gray's *The Agricultural Tractor, 1855–1950*, concerns the 1918 Kardell Utility. Nothing more is recorded, other than the name and the fact that it was built in St. Louis, Missouri. The term gradually came to be applied to the plethora of Ford-Ferguson look-a-likes that developed in the 1950s as Ferguson's patents ran out, although the term is seldom applied to the Ford-Ferguson itself.

Besides being squat and carrying mounted implements, the Ford-Ferguson defined the utility tractor in other ways as well. The operator sat low and well forward over the rear axle with his legs astride the transmission. No platform was used. With hydraulic controls, this much safer position was allowed since there was no need to reach back for implement handles. The front axle was similar to that of wide-front row-crops. It had downward-extending kingpins, rather than being straight across as on the standard tread machines. This feature gave the utility tractor the same crop clearance as wide-front row-crops. The rear axle of the utility tractor configuration generally did not incorporate any drop gearing. Wheel spacing was adjustable. Finally, the utility tractor was equally at home doing standard tread tractor work or row-crop work (up to the limitation of clearance). It was also generally capable of doing orchard work.

From 1939 through 1947, Deere averaged about 25,000 tractors per year for the small-farm market. This number included Models B, L, LA, and H. In the same time, Ford-Ferguson sold an average 42,000 per year of its only model. Deere and other marketing organizations saw the beginning of the trend away from the tricycle front end.

*Previous pages*
Introduced in 1947, the Model M was billed as a general-purpose utility tractor. This 1948 Model M is owned by Ken Koberg of Walcott, Iowa. *Andy Kraushaar*

The Ford 8N assembly line. At its peak, Ford was building over 400 of these tractors per day. The 8N (the "8" signifying 1948), was an update of the 9N, introduced in 1939. Ford and Ferguson had parted ways by then and were involved in a bitter lawsuit. Ferguson began building his own update of the 9N, the Ferguson TO-20. Thus began the proliferation of the squat utility tractor concept, which was to steer the industry away from the general-purpose row-crop configuration.
*Author Collection*

John Deere's answer to the Ford-Ferguson, the Model M. It was the first tractor produced in the new Dubuque tractor plant. Other than the previous small Models L and LA, it was the first Deere tractor with a driveshaft. The Model M was also the first Deere tractor to have the Touch-O-Matic hydraulic implement lift system. This nicely restored Model M is owned by Jim Kenney of Streater, Illinois. *Author Collection*

## The John Deere Model M

To counter Ford's inroad into the small farm marketplace, the John Deere Model M was born, replacing the L, LA, and the H. It was billed as a general-purpose utility tractor. The M came equipped with a gasoline-only vertical, relatively high-speed (1,650 rpm), two-cylinder engine—a departure from the customary horizontal transverse engine. It also had the Touch-O-Matic rear implement hydraulic lift. This was similar in function to the three-point hitch. It did not, however, incorporate Draft Control, as the situation with Ferguson's patents was still unclear.

The M's configuration was that of the Ford-Ferguson. With its vertical inline engine, a driveshaft was required to bring the power back to the transmission. A foot-operated clutch was used. These features had been pioneered on Deere tractors by the diminutive garden-type Models L and LA, which also had vertical, inline two-cylinder engines. The Model M and its successors were built in Deere's Dubuque plant.

By the end of the 1947 model year, Henry Ford II had abrogated the handshake agreement made by his grandfather and Harry Ferguson. He then began making an updated model called the 8N (for the year 1948). Ferguson, who had already begun making his own similar tractor in England (the Ferguson TE-20), set up an American factory to make an Americanized version, the TO-20. TE-20s were imported until 1949 while the new factory was coming up to speed. So, with the 8N, the TE-20, and the John Deere Model M, there were three bona fide utility tractors on the market in 1948. In 1951, Ferguson added an upgraded Model TO-30, Ford replaced the 8N with the Jubilee in 1953, and Oliver introduced the Model 55 in 1954. Other makers added rear hydraulic lifts to their regular tractors.

The M's configuration did not satisfy all of Deere's customers, however, so in traditional Deere fashion the MT was added to the line in 1949. The MT was essentially the same tractor but could be equipped with an adjustable wide front, dual tricycle front, or single front wheel. Dual Touch-O-Matic was an added option, allowing independent control of right- and left-side implements.

## Post-war Expansion

In support of the war effort, Deere & Company produced 75-millimeter cannon shells. To ensure a continuing supply, the army offered to share the cost of a new plant for their production. It was at this time that Charles Wiman returned from his stint in Washington, D.C., to retake the reins of the company, full of enthusiasm for postwar prospects. It was understood that this plant would be retained by Deere after the war. The company settled on Dubuque, Iowa, for the new plant. Dubuque was selected as being outside either the Moline or Waterloo labor markets, but yet close enough for ready control from Moline. Being on the Mississippi River also was a factor in choosing Dubuque.

Dubuque, then, became the home of Deere tractors with driveshafts, such as the Model M and those of its family that followed. Note that the other Deere tractors, made at Waterloo, had transverse engines that were geared directly into the transmissions. This production arrangement was continued until 1960, when the two-cylinder engine was discontinued.

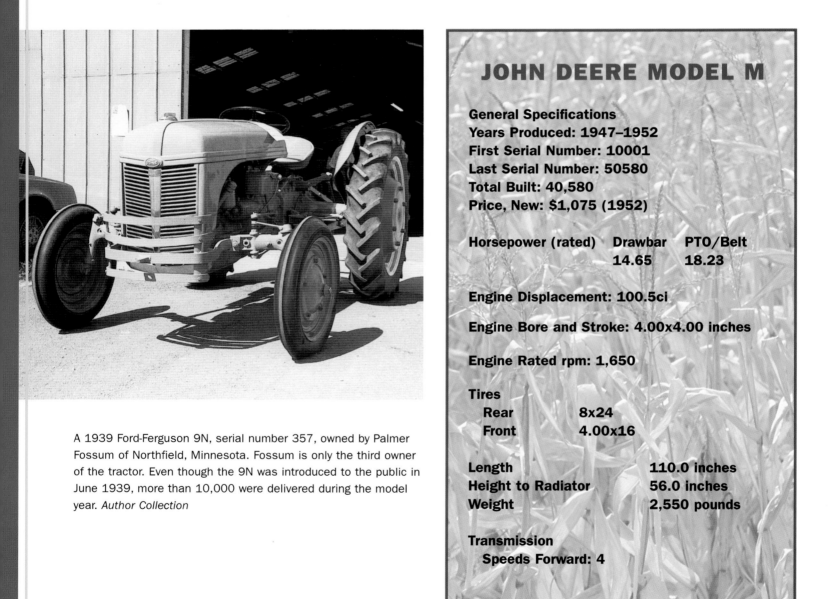

A 1939 Ford-Ferguson 9N, serial number 357, owned by Palmer Fossum of Northfield, Minnesota. Fossum is only the third owner of the tractor. Even though the 9N was introduced to the public in June 1939, more than 10,000 were delivered during the model year. *Author Collection*

# JOHN DEERE MODEL M

**General Specifications**
**Years Produced: 1947–1952**
**First Serial Number: 10001**
**Last Serial Number: 50580**
**Total Built: 40,580**
**Price, New: $1,075 (1952)**

| Horsepower (rated) | Drawbar | PTO/Belt |
|---|---|---|
| | 14.65 | 18.23 |

**Engine Displacement: 100.5ci**

**Engine Bore and Stroke: 4.00x4.00 inches**

**Engine Rated rpm: 1,650**

**Tires**
| | | |
|---|---|---|
| Rear | 8x24 | |
| Front | 4.00x16 | |

| | |
|---|---|
| Length | 110.0 inches |
| Height to Radiator | 56.0 inches |
| Weight | 2,550 pounds |

**Transmission**
  **Speeds Forward: 4**

An unstyled B, a 520, and a Model 50 on display at the 1992 Central States Thresherman's Reunion in Pontiac, Illinois. *Author Collection*

The start of the "Slow Race" at the 1992 Central States Thresherman's Reunion. Competing, left to right: a John Deere Model H, an Allis Chalmers Model G, a John Deere Model D, a John Deere Model M, and a John Deere Model 50. *Author Collection*

The end of the "Slow Race." The John Deere Model 50 is the hands-down winner. The owner said he did nothing to make it especially slow; that's just the way it is. The John Deere H and the Allis G are battling it out for second place, with the G eventually getting the nod. The John Deere M is out of it, as is the three-speed Model D, about 50 feet ahead when the operator killed the engine trying to make it run slower. *Author Collection*

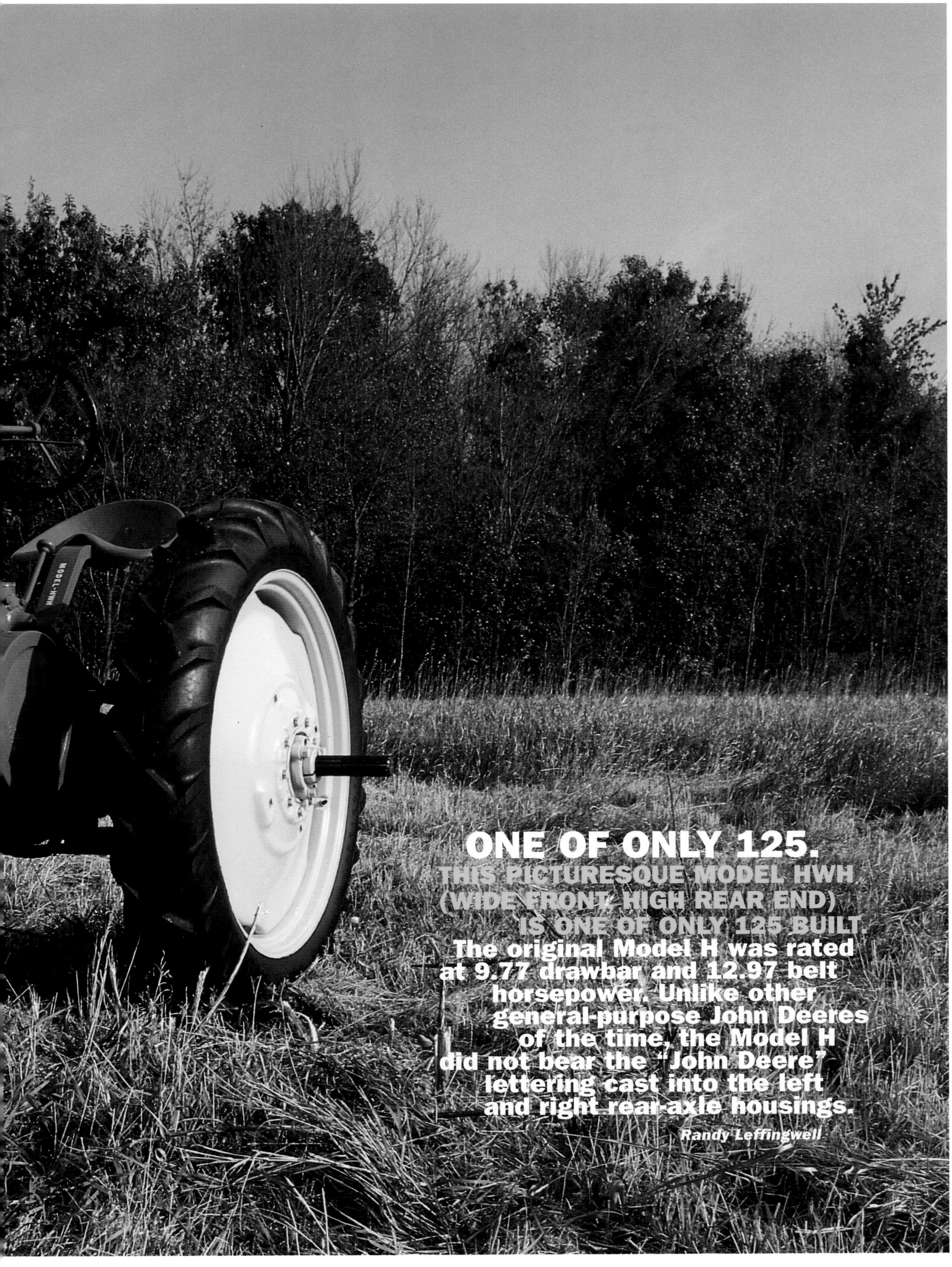

**ONE OF ONLY 125.**
THIS PICTURESQUE MODEL HWH
(WIDE FRONT, HIGH REAR END)
IS ONE OF ONLY 125 BUILT.
The original Model H was rated
at 9.77 drawbar and 12.97 belt
horsepower. Unlike other
general-purpose John Deeres
of the time, the Model H
did not bear the "John Deere"
lettering cast into the left
and right rear-axle housings.

*Randy Leffingwell*

THE MODEL M WAS **THE FIRST TRACTOR TO MAKE USE OF DEERE'S NEW TOUCH-O-MATIC HYDRAULIC SYSTEM.** The Model MT (tricycle), as seen here, more closely resembled the Model H than it did any earlier John Deere tractor. The MT was rated at 14.08 drawbar and 18.33 belt horsepower, and was produced from 1949 to 1952.

*Randy Leffingwell*

# Chapter Five

# THE GENERAL-PURPOSE TRACTOR MATURES

### The Numbered Series

When the need for increased power was recognized at Deere, there were also powerful influences within the company to do away with the two-cylinder engine. These influences included Charles Deere Wiman. The new tractor group at Dubuque that developed the vertical-engine Model M had also been experimenting with four-cylinder engines for combines. Wiman favored capitalizing on the group's progress. Nevertheless, the pent-up demand following the war mandated caution. Tractor sales were booming. Ultimately, there was not time to change engines, yet the competition clearly demanded upgrading.

Thus, in the1952 model year, the complete line was revised and improved (except for the fairly new Model R standard tread diesel). The new line of general-purpose tractors was announced as follows:
- The Model 40 replaced the M.
- The Model 50 replaced the B.
- The Model 60 replaced the A.
- The Model 70 replaced the G.

Power was increased across the board, plus there were improvements in styling and convenience. Deere's answer to the three-point hitch was universally available. Both hydraulics and PTO were now independent (or live).

The Model 40 was available only in a gasoline version, but later, an All-fuel (for distillate, tractor fuel, or gasoline) version was added. The others were available in gasoline, All-fuel, and LPG versions. In 1953, the diesel version of the mighty Model 70 was unveiled.

The changing of the rear wheel spacing for the new models was improved with a rack-and-pinion adjusting mechanism. Also new for the horizontal engine, a water pump and thermostat were added. For the first time, these tractors did not rely on the simple, effective, old-fashioned thermosyphon cooling system. With this change came smaller, higher-temperature, pressurized radiators. Gone were the manually operated radiator shutters.

With the introduction of the 50 and 60 tractors, the pressed-steel frame was replaced with a cast-steel frame of the type used before 1947. Other features of the new line included an improved seat, optional power steering (1954), a 12-volt electrical system, and lengthened clutch and throttle levers.

### The Three-Numbered 20 Series

By 1955, archrival International Harvester had restyled and renumbered its line of tractors. Not to be outdone, Deere, in mid-1956, also introduced restyled and renumbered tractors. A number 20 was added to the first number of each series; thus, the 40 became the 420, the 50 the 520, etc. At the same time, the Model 320, a new small general-purpose utility unit, was added.

The most striking feature of the new series was the yellow hood side panels, a change from the previous all-green sheet metal. The big news with the new series, however, was Custom Powr-Trol—Deere's version of Harry Ferguson's Draft Control. With Custom Powr-Trol, a new position-responsive rockshaft enabled the operator to preset working depth. He could then raise the implement for a turn at the row end and then drop it to the same working depth as before. Also featured was Load-and-Depth Control (Draft Control). The patents Ferguson held were now up for grabs following his settlement with Ford. This feature automatically applied raise pressure to lift the implement when tough soil conditions were encountered, thereby lessening the draft load and also pulling down on the back wheels to improve traction. Once the hard spot was passed, the system automatically returned the implement to its original depth.

Except for the diesel, the engines were all new. Power was increased 18 to 25 percent. Displacement increased, speed increased, and improved cylinder heads and pistons increased the power and reduced fuel consumption.

The science of ergonomics was used to increase the productivity of the tractor by increasing the productivity of the

The clutch side of the 50. The "hub cap" covering the unit can be popped off with a screwdriver, exposing the adjusting castellated nuts. The clutch is a multiple-disk type.

*Previous pages*
About 57,000 John Deere Model 60 row-crop tractors were built between 1952 and 1956. They originally sold for a little under $2,500. Not a bad price for a tractor with a base weight of 5,300 pounds.

*Opposite*
The flywheel side of Ramminger's Model 60. On the opposite side of the engine is the clutch in about the same position. Deere heavily advertised the advantages of the accessibility of these two elements. The flywheel is used for manual starting, and the clutch is readily disassembled for repair or replacement. Ramminger pointed out that it is the best policy to engage the clutch when the tractor is idling. One should never leave the transmission in gear with the clutch lever back. On their first John Deere tractor when Rich was a boy, they learned this the hard way and burned the clutch out in two weeks. His dad hung the plates on the wall as a reminder.

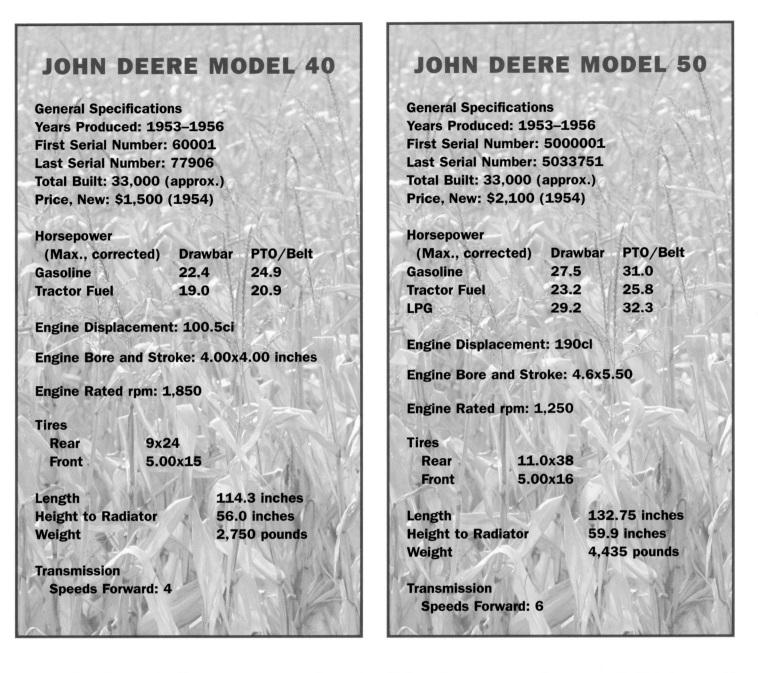

## JOHN DEERE MODEL 40

**General Specifications**
**Years Produced:** 1953–1956
**First Serial Number:** 60001
**Last Serial Number:** 77906
**Total Built:** 33,000 (approx.)
**Price, New:** $1,500 (1954)

**Horsepower**

| (Max., corrected) | Drawbar | PTO/Belt |
|---|---|---|
| Gasoline | 22.4 | 24.9 |
| Tractor Fuel | 19.0 | 20.9 |

**Engine Displacement:** 100.5ci

**Engine Bore and Stroke:** 4.00x4.00 inches

**Engine Rated rpm:** 1,850

**Tires**

| | |
|---|---|
| Rear | 9x24 |
| Front | 5.00x15 |

| | |
|---|---|
| Length | 114.3 inches |
| Height to Radiator | 56.0 inches |
| Weight | 2,750 pounds |

**Transmission**
Speeds Forward: 4

## JOHN DEERE MODEL 50

**General Specifications**
**Years Produced:** 1953–1956
**First Serial Number:** 5000001
**Last Serial Number:** 5033751
**Total Built:** 33,000 (approx.)
**Price, New:** $2,100 (1954)

**Horsepower**

| (Max., corrected) | Drawbar | PTO/Belt |
|---|---|---|
| Gasoline | 27.5 | 31.0 |
| Tractor Fuel | 23.2 | 25.8 |
| LPG | 29.2 | 32.3 |

**Engine Displacement:** 190cl

**Engine Bore and Stroke:** 4.6x5.50

**Engine Rated rpm:** 1,250

**Tires**

| | |
|---|---|
| Rear | 11.0x38 |
| Front | 5.00x16 |

| | |
|---|---|
| Length | 132.75 inches |
| Height to Radiator | 59.9 inches |
| Weight | 4,435 pounds |

**Transmission**
Speeds Forward: 6

operator. Therefore, on the 20 Series, operator comfort and convenience features were added. A new more roomy, "stand-at-will" platform was added, the instruments were easier to read, the controls fell more naturally to hand, and the new Float-Ride seat, supported on an adjustable rubber torsion spring and hydraulic shock absorber, was standard. Another new operator convenience was power-adjustable rear wheel spacing on most models.

The 320 was built to handle two l2-inch bottom plows. For some reason, the 320 was never tested at the University of Nebraska.

Now, with all the variations—general purpose, standard tread, orchard, utility general purpose, high-crop, and some of these with a choice of four different fuel engines—the number of distinct tractor offerings was staggering. For the most part, the competition was overwhelmed.

### The Three-Numbered 30 Series

After the broad range of improvements incorporated into the

20 Series just two years earlier, you would think there would not be much left for a new model. Competition in the tractor business was so intense, however, that refinements in the line were mandated. The 238-horsepower Steiger was born in 1957, indicating the trend of the future. Case, Minneapolis-Moline, and Oliver also introduced new capable diesels in 1957. New automatic transmissions were coming in, such as the Case-O-Matic and Ford's Select-O-Speed, as well as torque-amplifier step-down shifters on several competing brands; and the Oliver 995 had a torque converter.

John Deere, for its 30 series, concentrated on styling, safety, and comfort. New standard-equipment flat-topped fenders with handholds protected the operator from mud and dust, and from accidental contact with the tires. Besides the handholds, a convenient step in front of the axle made mounting and dismounting safer and easier. The fenders also incorporated a new lighting system for improved night work. A new angled instrument panel featured instruments clustered around the steering column, which projected upward at a more convenient angle. A 24-volt electric starting option was available in place of the V-4 pony motor on the new 730 diesel. And finally, all models had new quieter Oval Tone mufflers.

The last new John Deere two-cylinder tractor added to the line appeared in 1959. It was the Model 435 diesel. This version of the 430 series was powered by a two-cylinder version of the General Motors two-cycle supercharged diesel engine. This was the first John Deere tractor introduced after the adoption of industry PTO standards; as such, it was available with either a 1,000- or 540-rpm PTO. The 435 was available in only the row-crop utility configuration.

## The End of the Reign

Early in 1953, after the success of the two numbered series was assured, Deere management again turned its thoughts to tractor engines with more than two cylinders. The handwriting, they realized, was on the wall—despite their market niche and all the touted advantages of the two-cylinder engine, its limits had been reached. The question was not whether, but when, for the larger tractors. Another question was whether to switch only the diesels or to change the entire line at one time.

The two-cylinder engine was known for its simplicity, long life, and fuel economy; factors that are always requirements of a tractor engine. Eventually, however, as the 1960s approached,

John Deere management realized that the two-cylinder configuration was restricting design considerations. The advantages of cross-engine mounting—that is, straight spur gearing and belt pulley directly on the end of the crankshaft—no longer applied. Also, kerosene vaporizer manifolds and the like had been replaced by the diesel. Though the two-cylinder made a good diesel, the configuration offered no advantages. Further, much of the future of Deere's business would be in self-propelled combines and similar machines, and in individual diesel engine sales. Here, the large, heavy two-cylinder was at a disadvantage against a high-speed four-cylinder diesel. And finally, design limits were being reached as far as increasing horsepower was concerned, and Deere management could predict horsepower doubling and even tripling in the next decade. In 1960, after nearly a half a century, two-cylinder farm tractors were terminated in favor of the new three-, four-, and six-cylinder models.

The correct term should be "essentially terminated," as two-cylinder Model 730s were built for export throughout 1961. Also, 730s were built in Argentina until 1970. In addition, the vertical Dubuque-built two-cylinder was used in various applications as well as in industrial crawlers for several years after 1960.

The John Deere Model 50 was the successor to the venerable Model B. The 50 was built in year models 1952 through 1956. Like the Model 60, the 50 reverted to the angle-iron frame of pre-1947 models, rather than the pressed-steel frame of late-styled As and Bs.

**THIS PRISTINE 1955 JOHN DEERE MODEL 50** APPEARED AT THE 1988 TWO-CYLINDER EXPO AND ALSO IN THE BOOK *HOW JOHNNY POPPER REPLACED THE HORSE.* It is owned by Rich Ramminger, who has spent countless hours to bring it to it's impressive restored condition.

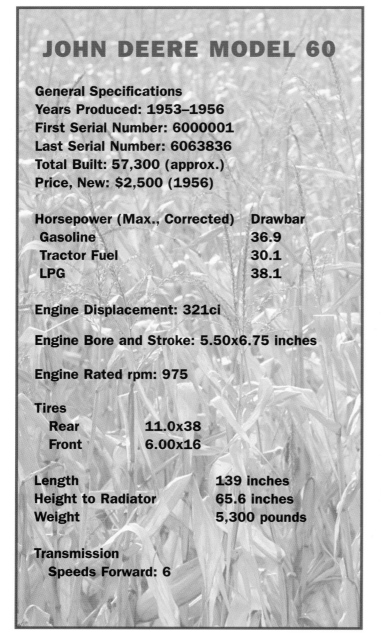

# JOHN DEERE MODEL 60

**General Specifications**
**Years Produced:** 1953–1956
**First Serial Number:** 6000001
**Last Serial Number:** 6063836
**Total Built:** 57,300 (approx.)
**Price, New:** $2,500 (1956)

| Horsepower (Max., Corrected) | Drawbar |
|---|---|
| Gasoline | 36.9 |
| Tractor Fuel | 30.1 |
| LPG | 38.1 |

**Engine Displacement:** 321ci

**Engine Bore and Stroke:** 5.50x6.75 inches

**Engine Rated rpm:** 975

| Tires | |
|---|---|
| Rear | 11.0x38 |
| Front | 6.00x16 |

| Length | 139 inches |
|---|---|
| Height to Radiator | 65.6 inches |
| Weight | 5,300 pounds |

**Transmission**
Speeds Forward: 6

Rich Ramminger's 1956 Model 60 is shown at 82-year-old Walter Manthe's farm in Arlington, Wisconsin. Walter, who was born on the place, got his first tractor in 1942: a John Deere B. The 65-acre spread supported a family of four.

The Roll-O-Matic narrow front was a John Deere exclusive. The two wheels were geared together in such a way that when one went up, the other went down. This allowed the individual tire to step over an obstacle, such as a rock, raising the front of the tractor only half as much. The result was much easier riding and steering and, as an added benefit, the system increased tire life.

*At right*
The Model 70 is the "no-neck" of the Deere row-crop line—big, strong, and born to pull! Yet it set a record for the least fuel consumption on a pounds-per-horsepower-hour basis at the University of Nebraska.

## JOHN DEERE MODEL 70

**General Specifications**
**Years Produced: 1953–1956**
**First Serial Number: 7000001**
**Last Serial Number: 7043757**
**Total Built: 43,000 (approx.)**
**Price, New: $2,800 (1955)**

**Horsepower**

| (Max., Corrected) | Drawbar | PTO/Belt |
|---|---|---|
| Gasoline | 44.2 | 50.4 |
| Tractor Fuel | 41.0 | 45.0 |
| LPG | 46.1 | 52.0 |
| Diesel | 45.7 | 51.5 |

**Engine Displacement:**

| | |
|---|---|
| Gasoline and LPG | 379.5ci |
| All-fuel | 412.5 |
| Diesel | 376.0 |

| Engine Rated rpm: | 975 |
|---|---|
| Diesel | 1,125 |

**Tires**

| Rear | 12.0x38 |
|---|---|
| Front | 6.00x16 |

| Length | 134.6 inches |
|---|---|
| Height to Radiator | 65.6 inches |
| Weight (gasoline) | 6,035 pounds |

**Transmission**
    Speeds Forward: 6

A Model 70 hi-crop LP; one of only 25 made. This one is owned by Norman Smith of Carrolton, Illinois. The tractor originally sold for the price of a new Pontiac, but to get Smith's attention today, you'd have to be bringing the price of a new Jaguar or Porsche.

**SERENDIPITY ABOUNDS—**
LYLE PALS BOUGHT THIS MODEL 70 DIESEL, SERIAL NUMBER 7036203, TWICE. The second time, Pals found it on a trailer heading for a scrap yard! Not only did the Model 70 provide ample horsepower, it broke a long-standing fuel economy record in Nebraska testing.

A 1956 John Deere Model 70 diesel with pony motor start. This one is owned by Rich Ramminger of Morrisonville, Wisconsin. Although it appears to be a fresh restoration, Ramminger did the work about 10 years ago and has worked the tractor about 150 hours since. Ramminger plowed with it during the spring of the year this picture was taken.

*Opposite*
The instrument panel of a pony motor start Model 70 diesel has functions for both the pony motor and the diesel itself. By 1953, when the Model 70 came out, instrument panels were much more complete than in the early days of general-purpose tractors.

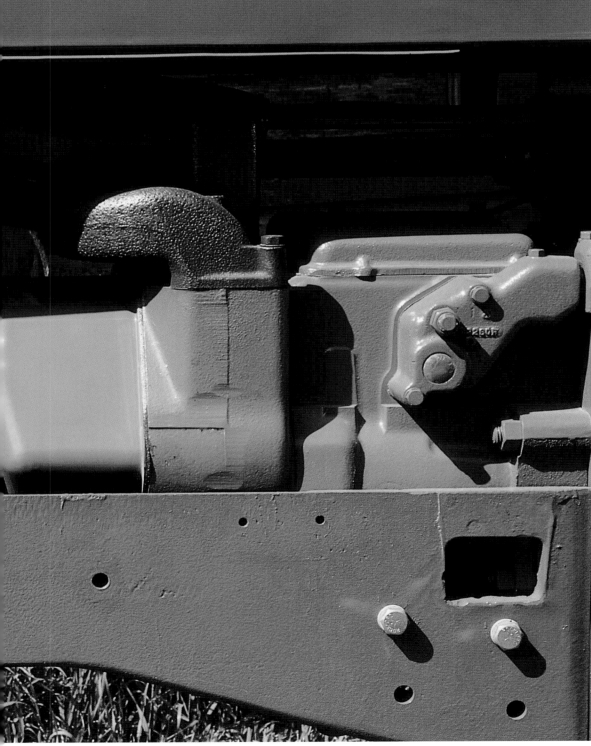

The Model 70 diesel was Deere's first row-crop diesel tractor. It came with a V-4 pony-motor starter. Exhaust heat from the pony was routed through the diesel to warm them up for starting. Shown is Rich Ramminger's 1956 model.

The view from above shows the rugged lines of this 1956 Model 70 diesel. Starting power was provided by an 18.8-ci V-4 pony motor. The basic weight of the Model 70 was over 6,500 pounds. With ballast, that weight can double.

The John Deere Model 320 was introduced as part of the 20 series in 1956. It was rated as a one- or two-plow tractor. This one is equipped with the later angled steering wheel instead of the vertical wheel of the original 320s.

THE 20 SERIES SPORTED A FLASHY NEW PAINT JOB WITH BRIGHT YELLOW ON THE HOOD AND GRILLE. **CERTAINLY ONE OF THE NEATEST COLLECTOR TRACTORS OF ALL TIME,** THIS MODEL 320 REPRESENTS THE BEST OF THE LATER TWO-CYLINDERS IN A SMALL PACKAGE.

# JOHN DEERE MODEL 320

**General Specifications**
**Years Produced:** 1956–1958
**First Serial Number:** 320001
**Last Serial Number:** 325518
**Total Built:** 3,083 (approx.)
**Price, New:** $1,970 (1958)

**Horsepower**

| (Max., Corrected) | Drawbar | PTO/Belt |
|---|---|---|
| Gasoline | 22.4 | 24.9 |

**Engine Displacement:** 100.5ci

**Engine Bore and Stroke:** 4.00x4.00 inches

**Engine Rated rpm:** 1,850

**Tires**
| | |
|---|---|
| Rear | 9x24 |
| Front | 5.00x15 |

| | |
|---|---|
| Length | 119.3 inches (RCU) |
| Height to Radiator | 50 inches |
| Weight | 2,750 pounds |

**Transmission**
  Speeds Forward: 4

The Model 320 is fairly rare with only about 3,000 built between 1956 and 1958. It had the 100.5-ci engine of the Model 40 rather than the new 113.5-ci engine of the 420. The price difference of only about $400 caused most farmers to opt for the capability of the larger engine.

A 420H (hi-crop) tractor operates with a sprayer in an alfalfa field. The 420 employed a vertical two-cylinder engine. Like other Deere tractors with vertical engines, it was made in Dubuque. *Deere Archives*

A row-crop utility version of the John Deere 420 tractor. Although the Dubuque line of vertical-engined two-cylinder tractors began life on the low end of Deere's horsepower spectrum with the Model M, power was up to 30 horsepower on the PTO by the time the 420 came along. *Deere Archives*

## JOHN DEERE MODEL 420

**General Specifications**
**Years Produced:** 1953–1956
**First Serial Number:** 8000001
**Last Serial Number:** 8136868
**Total Built:** 55,000 (approx.)
**Price, New:** $2,300 (1958)

**Horsepower**

| (Max., Corrected) | Drawbar | PTO/Belt |
|---|---|---|
| Gasoline | 27.1 | 29.2 |
| Tractor Fuel | 21.9 | 23.5 |
| LPG | 28.0 | 30.0 |

**Engine Displacement: 113ci**

**Engine Bore and Stroke: 4.25x4.00 inches**

| **Engine Rated rpm:** | 1,850 |
|---|---|

**Tires**

| Rear | 9x24 |
|---|---|
| Front | 5.00x15 |

| Length | 119.3 inches (RCU) |
|---|---|
| Height to Radiator | 56 inches |
| Weight | 3,250 pounds |

**Transmission**
  **Speeds Forward:** 4 (5 optional)

# JOHN DEERE MODEL 620

**General Specifications**
**Years Produced:** 1956–1958
**First Serial Number:** 6200000
**Last Serial Number:** 6222686
**Total Built:** 22,600 (approx.)
**Price, New:** $3,000 (1956)

**Horsepower**

| (Max., Corrected) | Drawbar | PTO/Belt |
| --- | --- | --- |
| Gasoline | 44.2 | 48.7 |
| Tractor Fuel | 32.7 | 35.7 |
| LPG | 45.8 | 50.3 |

**Engine Bore and Stroke:** 5.50x6.75 inches

**Engine Rated rpm:** 1,125

**Tires**

| | |
| --- | --- |
| Rear | 12.4x38 |
| Front | 6.00x16 |

| | |
| --- | --- |
| **Length** | 135.25 inches |
| **Height to Radiator** | 66 inches |
| **Weight (gasoline)** | 5,900 pounds |

**Transmission**
   Speeds Forward: 6

A typical setting for the John Deere 620 row-crop tractor. This one is pulling a Model 494 planter with a dry fertilizer attachment. The 620 was made between 1956 and 1958. *Deere Archives*

The mighty 720S LP. With a 361-ci two-cylinder engine operating on LPG, it could produce a maximum of 60 PTO horsepower. Of the 3,000 720Ss built, very few had the LP option and are now much sought-after by collectors. *Author Collection*

# JOHN DEERE MODEL 720

**General Specifications**
**Years Produced:** 1956–1958
**First Serial Number:** 7200000
**Last Serial Number:** 7229002
**Total Built:** 29,000 (approx.)
**Price, New:** $3,700 (1958)

**Horsepower**

| (Max., Corrected) | Drawbar | PTO/Belt |
| --- | --- | --- |
| Gasoline | 53.0 | 59.1 |
| Tractor Fuel | 41.3 | 45.3 |
| LPG | 54.2 | 59.6 |
| Diesel | 53.7 | 58.8 |

**Engine Displacement:**

| | |
| --- | --- |
| Gasoline and LPG | 360.5ci |
| All-fuel | 360.5ci |
| Diesel | 376.0ci |

**Engine Rated rpm:** 1,125

**Tires**

| | |
| --- | --- |
| Rear | 12.4x38 |
| Front | 6.00x16 |

| | |
| --- | --- |
| **Length** | 134.6 inches |
| **Height to Radiator** | 65.6 inches |
| **Weight (gasoline)** | 6,790 pounds |

**Transmission Speeds Forward:** 6

Orv Rothgarn's Model 520. The 520 was introduced in 1956 and production continued into 1958. It was advertised at 26 drawbar horsepower and 32 PTO horsepower!

# JOHN DEERE MODEL 330

**General Specifications**
**Years Produced:** 1958–1960
**First Serial Number:** 330001
**Last Serial Number:** 331091
**Total Built:** 1,000 (approx.)
**Price, New:** $2,200 (1960)

**Horsepower**

| (Max., Corrected) | Drawbar | PTO/Belt |
|---|---|---|
| Gasoline | 22.4 | 24,9 |

**Engine Displacement:** 100.5ci

**Engine Bore and Stroke:** 4.00x4.00 inches

**Engine Rated rpm:** 1,500

**Tires**

| | |
|---|---|
| Rear | 9x24 |
| Front | 5.00x15 |

| | |
|---|---|
| Length | 119.3 inches (RCU) |
| Height to Radiator | 50 inches |
| Weight | 2,750 pounds |

**Transmission**
  Speeds Forward: 4

Powering a mower and a hay conditioner were normal tasks for this John Deere Model 330 tractor. It was essentially the same as the previous 320, but the steering wheel was placed at a more convenient angle. *Deere Archives*

The 430 also came in an LP model. This one is shown with a 5-foot disk at a Deere experimental farm. *Deere Archives*

The GM diesel engine powering the John Deere 435 tractor is a two-cycle, two-cylinder unit with a roots-type blower. Produced only in 1959 and only in the row-crop utility version, the 435 is fairly rare for such a late year model (less than 5,000 were built). The 435 is capable of a maximum PTO horsepower of 32.9, according to tests at the University of Nebraska. The Model 435 was the first John Deere to adopt the 1,000-rpm PTO speed standard. Owner Lyle Pals says he uses ether for starting even in the summer.

# JOHN DEERE
# MODEL 430

**General Specifications**
**Years Produced: 1958–1960**
**First Serial Number: 140001**
**Last Serial Number: 161096**
**Total Built: 12,680 (approx.)**
**Price, New: $2,500 (1960)**

**Horsepower**

| (Max., Corrected) | Drawbar | PTO/Belt |
|---|---|---|
| Gasoline | 27.1 | 29.2 |
| Tractor Fuel | 21.9 | 23.5 |
| LPG | 28.0 | 30.0 |

**Engine Displacement: 113ci**

**Engine Bore and Stroke: 4.25x4.00 inches**

**Engine Rated rpm: 1,850**

**Tires**

| Rear | 9x24 |
|---|---|
| Front | 5.00x15 |

| Length | 119.3 inches |
|---|---|
| Height to Radiator | 56 inches |
| Weight | 3,250 pounds |

**Transmission**
    **Speeds Forward: 4 (5 optional)**
    **Direction Reverser optional**

# JOHN DEERE MODEL 435

**General Specifications**
**Years Produced: 1959–1960**
**First Serial Number: 435001**
**Last Serial Number: 439626**
**Total Built: 4,500 (approx.)**
**Price, New: $3,000 (1958)**

| Horsepower | Drawbar | PTO/Belt |
|---|---|---|
| (Max., Corrected) | 27.6 | 32.9 |

**Engine Displacement: 106ci**

**Engine Bore and Stroke: 4.87x4.50 inches**

**Engine Rated rpm: 1,850**

**Tires**
| | |
|---|---|
| Rear | 13.6x28 |
| Front | 6.00x16 |

| | |
|---|---|
| Length | 119.3 inches |
| Height to Radiator | 56 inches |
| Weight | 4,000 pounds |

**Transmission**
   Speeds Forward: 4 (5 optional)
   Direction Reverser optional

The last of the two-cylinders, the Model 435. Produced only in 1959, the 435 employed a supercharged General Motors 2-53 two-cycle diesel engine. This one, serial number 436200, is owned by Lyle Pals of Egan, Illinois. Lyle says you drive it like you want to kill it, in reference to the requirement to keep the rpm up so that the supercharger does its job. Also, since it is a two-cycle, it sounds like it is going twice as fast as it actually is.

# JOHN DEERE MODEL 530

**General Specifications**
**Years Produced: 1958–1960**
**First Serial Number: 5300000**
**Last Serial Number: 5309814**
**Total Built: 9,800 (approx.)**
**Price, New: $2,400 (1960)**

**Horsepower**

| (Max., Corrected) | Drawbar | PTO/Belt |
|---|---|---|
| Gasoline | 34.3 | 38.6 |
| Tractor Fuel | 24.8 | 26.6 |
| LPG | 34.2 | 38.1 |

**Engine Displacement: 321ci**

**Engine Bore and Stroke: 5.50x6.75 inches**

**Engine Rated rpm: 1,125**

**Tires**

| | |
|---|---|
| Rear | 12.4x36 |
| Front | 5.50x16 |

| | |
|---|---|
| Length | 132.75 inches |
| Height to Radiator | 66 inches |
| Weight | 5,900 pounds |

**Transmission**
   **Speeds Forward: 6**

Lyle Pals' 530 has the Custom Powr-Trol load-compensating three-point hitch. It also has dished rear wheel weights, Deere part number F 1478 L and R.

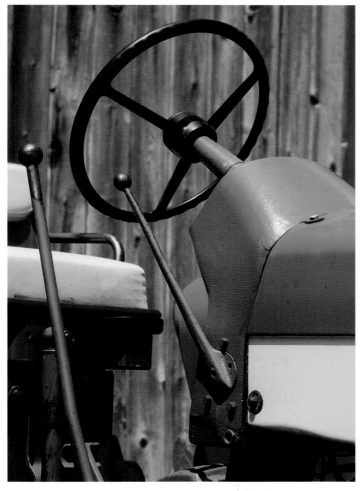

The 30 series boasted convenient controls. Shown is the "office" of a 630. The throttle lever is on the side of the cowling; the other, longer lever is the clutch.

The well-worn clutch housing of this Model 630 attests to many hours of use. The brakepad mechanism is for stopping the downstream half of the clutch from rotating by its own flywheel effect to enable the shifting of gears.

Orv Rothgarn of Owatonna, Minnesota, is a typical John Deere collector. He has 23 John Deere tractors, including this 630. He does some farming and landscaping (using two Ford Ns and a John Deere M) and is a retired lathe supervisor at the Owatonna Tool Company.

*Opposite*
Lyle Pals' 530 is serial number 530930, a 1958 model. Note the big Oval Tone muffler, which characterized the 30-series tractors.

# JOHN DEERE MODEL 630

**General Specifications**
Years Produced: 1958–1960
First Serial Number: 6300000
Last Serial Number: 6317201
Total Built: 18,000 (approx.)
Price, New: $3,300 (1958)

**Horsepower**

| (Max., Corrected) | Drawbar | PTO/Belt |
|---|---|---|
| Gasoline | 44.2 | 48.7 |
| Tractor Fuel | 32.7 | 35.7 |
| LPG | 45.8 | 50.3 |

Engine Displacement: 321ci

Engine Bore and Stroke: 5.50x6.75 inches

Engine Rated rpm: 1,125

**Tires**

| Rear | 12.4x38 |
|---|---|
| Front | 6.00x16 |

| Length | 135.25 inches |
|---|---|
| Height to Radiator | 66 inches |
| Weight | 5,900 pounds |

**Transmission**
Speeds Forward: 6

Although over 30 years old, this 630 is still much in demand by farmers for routine farm chores. A new 40- to 50-horsepower tractor would cost three to four times as much as a good refurbished 630. Plus, with the 630, you get the distinctive sound of the two-cylinder engine.

# JOHN DEERE
# MODEL 730

**General Specifications**
Years Produced: 1958–1960
First Serial Number: 7300000
Last Serial Number: 7330358
Total Built: 30,000 (approx.)
Price, New: $3,700 (1960)

**Horsepower**

| (Max., Corrected) | Drawbar | PTO/Belt |
|---|---|---|
| Gasoline | 53.0 | 59.1 |
| Tractor Fuel | 41.3 | 45.3 |
| LPG | 54.2 | 59.6 |
| Diesel | 53.7 | 58.8 |

**Engine Displacement:**

| | |
|---|---|
| Gasoline and LPG | 360.5ci |
| All-fuel | 360.5ci |
| Diesel | 376.0ci |

**Engine Rated rpm: 1,125**

**Tires**

| | |
|---|---|
| Rear | 12x38 |
| Front | 6.00x16 |

| | |
|---|---|
| Length | 134.6 inches |
| Height to Radiator | 65.6 inches |
| Weight (gasoline) | 6,790 pounds |

**Transmission**
Speeds Forward: 6

This placard on the Float-Ride seat of a John Deere 730 explains the proper settings for different driver weight categories.

The Float-Ride seat of this Model 730 can be adjusted to the weight of the operator.

A 1960 John Deere Model 730 standard. This photo was taken at the John Deere homestead in Grand Detour, Illinois.

A 1959 John Deere 730 row-crop (gasoline). The dual headlights in each fender enhanced night operations. The flat-top fenders protected the operator. Orv Rothgarn of Owatonna, Minnesota, owns this tractor.

ALTHOUGH **NEARLY 90 PERCENT OF MODEL 730S HAVE POWER STEERING, IT WAS NOT A FACTORY-STANDARD FEATURE.** The dual lights in each fender greatly enhance night operations for this 50-horsepower Model 730. The flat-top fenders protect the operator from contact with the tire and from dust and mud. Note the hydraulic snubber on the front of the Float-Ride seat.

# Appendix
# Competitive Analyses

**Notes on abbreviations used in tables:**

**Fuel:**   **K** = Kerosene
    **Dis**. = Distillate
    **D** = Diesel
    **G** = Gasoline

**Belt Horsepower:** From Test D. If the generator, hydraulic pump, etc., were not standard equipment, they were removed for these tests.

**Drawbar Horsepower:** Taken from Test H data, it is based on rated drawbar pull and speed. The difference between this and PTO horsepower is due to slippage, and to the power required to move the tractor itself.

The heavier the tractor, the less the slippage, but the more power required to move the tractor. Factory engineers looked for the ideal compromise.

**Pull:** Test G. The maximum drawbar pull in pounds.

**Fuel Consumption:** The rate of fuel consumption in horsepower hours per gallon taken from Test C conditions. The higher the number, the better.

**Weight:** The weight of the tractor plus ballast in pounds. Ballast was often added for Test G and other heavy pulling tests, and then removed for other tests to improve performance.

**Wheels:** Steel (S) or rubber (R)

# ROW CROP TRACTORS 1934–1936

|  | John Deere A | Farmall F-20 | A-C WC | Oliver 70 | Massey Chlngr | MM JT |
|---|---|---|---|---|---|---|
| Engine Displacement | 309 | 221 | 201 | 201 | 248 | 196 |
| Rated rpm | 975 | 1200 | 1300 | 1500 | 1200 | 1275 |
| Weight | 4059 | 4500 | 3792 | 3500 | 4200 | 3880 |
| Belt Horsepower | 23.6 | 22.2 | 21.5 | 25.3 | 26.2 | 21.9 |
| Drawbar Horsepower | 18.7 | 15.4 | 12.1 | 17 | 16.3 | 14.8 |
| Maximum Pull | 2923 | 2334 |  | 3120 | 2883 | 2787 |
| Fuel Consumption | 10.5 | 10.5 | 10.2 | 11.1 | 10.1 | 10.5 |
| Transmission Speeds | 4 | 4 | 4 | 4 | 4 | 4 |
| Fuel Type | K | K | K | G | Dis. | Dis. |
| Wheel Type | S | S | R | S | S | S |
| Test Number | 222 | 221 | 223 | 252 | 265 | 233 |

# ROW CROP TRACTORS 1947–1952

|  | John Deere A | Farmall M | Oliver 77 | MM Z | A-C WD |
|---|---|---|---|---|---|
| Engine Displacement | 321 | 248 | 194 | 206 | 201 |
| Rated rpm | 975 | 1450 | 1600 | 1500 | 1400 |
| Weight | 5228 | 6770 | 8012 | 5810 | 6057 |
| Belt Horsepower | 33.8 | 31.3 | 33 | 31.6 | 30.6 |
| Drawbar Horsepower | 26.7 | 24.9 | 25.8 | 25.2 | 23.6 |
| Maximum Pull | 4034 | 4365 | 4714 | 3498 | 4304 |
| Fuel Consumption | 11.4 | 12.5 | 11.7 | 10.7 | 11.8 |
| Transmission Speeds | 6 | 5 | 6 | 5 | 4 |
| Fuel Type | G | Dis. | G | G | G |
| Wheel Type | R | R | R | R | R |
| Test Number | 384 | 327 | 425 | 438 | 440 |

# ROW-CROP TRACTORS 1935–1937

|  | John Deere B | Farmall F-12 | Fordson A' Around | Case RC | MM ZT |
|---|---|---|---|---|---|
| Engine Displacement | 149 | 113 | 267 | 132 | 186 |
| Rated rpm | 1150 | 1400 | 1100 | 1425 | 1500 |
| Weight | 3275 | 3280 | 4020 | 3350 | 4280 |
| Belt Horsepower | 14.3 | 14.6 | 20.3 | 17.6 | 23.6 |
| Drawbar Horsepower | 9.8 | 10.1 | 11.9 | 11.6 | 16 |
| Maximum Pull | 1728 | 1870 | 1409 | 2103 | 3262 |
| Fuel Consumption | 10.2 | 9.5 | 7.7 | 9.7 | 10.1 |
| Transmission Speeds | 4 | 3 | 3 | 3 | 5 |
| Fuel Type | K | K | K | G | Dis. |
| Wheel Type | S | S | S | R | R |
| Test Number | 232 | 212 | 282 | 251 | 290 |

# ROW-CROP TRACTORS 1947–1952

|  | John Deere B | Farmall Super C | Oliver 66D | MM R | Massey 30 RT |
|---|---|---|---|---|---|
| Engine Displacement | 190 | 123 | 129 | 165 | 162 |
| Rated rpm | 1250 | 1650 | 1600 | 1500 | 1500 |
| Weight | 4400 | 5041 | 5717 | 4920 | 5265 |
| Belt Horsepower | 24.5 | 20.8 | 22.5 | 23.8 | 30.1 |
| Drawbar Horsepower | 19.1 | 16.3 | 17.7 | 18.3 | 20.6 |
| Maximum Pull | 3353 | n/a | 3571 | 2801 | 3273 |
| Fuel Consumption | 11.8 | 10.8 | 14.2 | 10.1 | 11.1 |
| Transmission Speeds | 6 | 4 | 6 | 4 | 5 |
| Fuel Type | G | G | D | G | G |
| Wheel Type | R | R | R | R | R |
| Test Number | 380 | 458 | 467 | 468 | 409 |

# 1947–1954

| | John Deere M | Ford 8N | Ferguson TE-20 | Oliver 55 | Ferguson TE-30 |
|---|---|---|---|---|---|
| Engine Displacement | 100.5 | 120 | 120 | 144 | 129 |
| Rated rpm | 1650 | 1750 | 1750 | 2000 | 1750 |
| Weight Tested | 2695 | 4043 | 4268 | 5501 | 4211 |
| Maximum PTO Horsepower | 19.5 | 26.2 | 24 | 34.4 | 29.3 |
| Maximum Drawbar Horsepower | 17.5 (est.) | 20.8 | 22.6 | 29.6 | 24.4 |
| Fuel Consumption * | 11.1 | 10.1 | 10.3 | 10.1 | 10 |
| Transmission Speeds | 4 | 4 | 4 | 6 | 4 |
| Fuel Type | G | G | G | G | G |
| Test Number | 387 | 443 | 392 | 524 | 466 |

* 10 hour run @ rated load.

# 1953–1956

| | John Deere 40 | John Deere 50 | John Deere 60 | John Deere 70 |
|---|---|---|---|---|
| Engine Displacement | 100.5 | 190 | 321 | 380 |
| Rated rpm | 1850 | 1250 | 975 | 975 |
| Weight Tested | 4569 | 5433 | 7405 | 8677 |
| Maximum PTO Horsepower | 23.5 | 28.9 | 38.6 | 45.9 |
| Rated Drawbar Horsepower | 17.4 | 20.9 | 28 | 33.6 |
| Fuel Consumption * | 9.4 | 10.5 | 10.2 | 10.3 |
| Transmission Speeds | 4 | 6 | 6 | 6 |
| Fuel Type | G | G | G | G |
| Test Number | 503 | 486 | 472 | 493 |

* 10 hour test @ rated drawbar power, horsepower hours per gallon.

# 1953–1956

| | Farmall Super M | Ford Jubilee | Case SC | Massey Pacer | Farmall Super H |
|---|---|---|---|---|---|
| Engine Displacement | 264 | 134 | 165 | 91 | 164 |
| Rated rpm | 1450 | 2000 | 1600 | 1800 | 1650 |
| Weight Tested | 8929 | 4389 | 6213 | 3469 | 6713 |
| Maximum PTO Horsepower | 43.9 | 30.2 | 23.7 | 17.9 | 31.3 |
| Rated Drawbar Horsepower | 33.3 | 20.2 | 18.5 | 13 | 23.5 |
| Fuel Consumption * | 10.3 | 10.1 | 9.4 | 9.3 | 10.3 |
| Transmission Speeds | 5 | 4 | 4 | 3 | 5 |
| Fuel Type | G | G | TracFuel | G | G |
| Test Number | 475 | 494 | 497 | 531 | 492 |

* 10 hour test @ rated drawbar power, horsepower hours per gallon.

# 1956–1958

| | John Deere 420 | John Deere 520 | John Deere 620 | John Deere 720 |
|---|---|---|---|---|
| Engine Displacement | 113 | 190 | 303 | 376 |
| Rated rpm | 1850 | 1325 | 1125 | 1125 |
| Weight Tested | 5781 | 6505 | 8655 | 9237 |
| Maximum PTO Horsepower | 27.3 | 36.1 | 44.3 | 56.7 |
| Rated Drawbar Horsepower | 20.8 | 26.1 | 33.6 | 40.4 |
| Fuel Consumption * | 9.7 | 11.1 | 11.3 | 16.6 |
| Transmission Speeds | 4 | 6 | 6 | 6 |
| Fuel Type | G | G | G | D |
| Test Number | 599 | 597 | 598 | 594 |

* 10 hour test @ rated drawbar power, horsepower hours per gallon.

# 1956–1958

| | Farmall 300 | Ford 960 | MM 455 | Oliver Sup 88 | Farmall 400 |
|---|---|---|---|---|---|
| Engine Displacement | 169 | 172 | 206 | 265 | 281 |
| Rated rpm | 1750 | 2200 | 1550 | 1600 | 1450 |
| Weight Tested | 8257 | 6156 | 6423 | 9446 | 9263 |
| Maximum PTO Horsepower | 36 | 44.1 | 40 | 54.9 | 48.8 |
| Rated Drawbar Horsepower | 27 | 30.7 | 31.2 | 37.9 | 34.7 |
| Fuel Consumption * | 9.6 | 10.3 | 10.6 | 13.4 | 12.8 |
| Transmission Speeds | 5 | 5 | 10 | 6 | 10 |
| Fuel Type | G | G | G | D | D |
| Test Number | 538 | 569 | 579 | 527 | 608 |

* 10 hour test @ rated drawbar power, horsepower hours per gallon,

# Index